Utopia or Bust

The Jacobin series features short interrogations of politics, economics, and culture from a socialist perspective, as an avenue to radical political practice. The books offer critical analysis and engagement with the history and ideas of the Left in an accessible format.

The series is a collaboration between Verso Books and *Jacobin* magazine, which is published quarterly in print and online at jacobinmag.com.

Other titles in this series available from Verso Books:

Playing the Whore by Melissa Gira Grant
Strike for America by Micah Vetricht

Utopia or Bust

A Guide to the Present Crisis

by
BENJAMIN KUNKEL

VERSO

London • New York

First published by Verso 2014
© Benjamin Kunkel 2014

Chapters 1, 2, 4, and 6 appeared first, in slightly different form,
in the *London Review of Books* (February 3, 2011; April 22,
2010; 4, May 10, 2012; August 8, 2013 respectively).
Chapter 3 appeared first in *n+1* (June 4, 2010).
Chapter 5 appeared first in the *New Statesman* (September 27, 2012).

1 3 5 7 9 10 8 6 4 2

Verso
UK: 6 Meard Street, London W1F 0EG
US: 20 Jay Street, Suite 1010, Brooklyn, NY 11201
www.versobooks.com

Verso is the imprint of New Left Books

ISBN-13: 978-1-78168-327-9 (PBK)
eISBN-13: 978-1-78168-328-6 (US)
eISBN-13: 978-1-78168-637-9 (UK)

British Library Cataloguing in Publication Data
A catalogue record for this book is available from the British Library

Library of Congress Cataloging-in-Publication Data
A catalog record for this book is available from the Library of Congress

Typeset in Fournier MT by Hewer Text UK Ltd, Edinburgh
Printed in the US by Maple Press

For
who can use it

It was thenceforth no longer a question whether this theorem or that was true, but whether it was useful to capital or harmful, expedient or inexpedient, politically dangerous or not. In place of disinterested inquirers, there were hired prize fighters; in place of genuine scientific research, the bad conscience and the evil intent of apologetic.

—Karl Marx, afterword to the second German edition of *Capital*

What ever happened to Political Economy, leaving me here?

—John Berryman, "Dream Song 84"

Contents

Introduction

To the disappointment of friends who would prefer to read my fiction—as well as of my literary agent, who would prefer to *sell* it—I seem to have become a Marxist public intellectual. Making matters worse, the relevant public has been a small one consisting of readers of the two publications, the *London Review of Books* and *n+1*, where all but one of the essays here first appeared, and my self-appointed role has likewise been modest. The essays attempt no original contribution to Marxist, or what you might call Marxish, thought. They simply offer basic introductions, with some critical comments, to a handful of contemporary thinkers on the left: three Marxists at work in their respective fields of geography, history, and cultural criticism; an anthropologist of anarchist convictions; and two philosophers who might be called neo-communists. These are meanwhile only a few of the present-day figures most attractive or interesting to me, and even if my discussion of their work does something to clarify the economic and cultural features of the ongoing capitalist crisis, several of the book's deficiencies will be more readily apparent than this achievement. The essays here no more than allude to the ecological and political dimensions of the crisis that burst into view in 2008, and they ignore altogether its uneven impact on different countries, genders, generations, "races."

The purpose of this modest explanatory volume is nevertheless immodest. The idea is to contribute something in the way of intellectual orientation to the project of replacing a capitalism bent on social polarization, the hollowing out of democracy, and ecological ruin with another, better order. This would be one adapted to collective survival and well-being, and marked by public ownership of important economic and financial institutions, by real as well as formal democratic capacities, and by social equality—all of which together would promise a renewal of culture in both the narrowly aesthetic and the broadly anthropological meanings of the term.

Theory, and writing about theorists, brings no victories by itself. Nor is there any need for everyone on the left or moving leftwards to converge on the same understanding of "late" capitalism, in the sense of recent or in decline, before anything can be done to make it "late" as in recently departed. Imperfect understanding is the lot of all political actors. Still, for at least a generation now, not only the broad public but many radicals themselves have felt uncertain that the left possessed a basic analysis of contemporary capitalism, let alone a program for its replacement. This intellectual disorientation has thinned our ranks and abetted our organizational disarray. Over the same period the comparative ideological coherence of our neoliberal opponents gave them an invaluable advantage in securing public assent to their policies or, failing that, resignation. Gaining a clearer idea of the present system should help us to challenge and one day overcome it. The essays in this short book about a number of other books, several of them long and dense, are collected here for whatever they can add to the effort. Social injustice and economic insecurity—bland terms for the calamities they name—would make overcoming capitalism urgent enough even if the system could boast a stable ecological footing; obviously, it cannot.

The odds of political success may not look particularly good at the moment. But the defects of global capitalism have become so plain to the eye—if still, for many minds, too mysterious in their causes and too inevitable in their effects— that the odds appear better than a few years ago. The crisis has not only sharpened anxieties but introduced new hopes, most spectacularly in 2011, year of the Arab Spring, of huge indignant crowds in European plazas, and of Occupy Wall Street. Today as I write in the summer of 2013, kindred movements have emerged, massively and spontaneously, in the streets of Turkey and Brazil. Over recent years my own political excitement, anxious and optimistic at once, has led to me to spend as much time thinking about global capitalism and its theorists as about the fictional characters in whose company I'd expected, as a novelist, to spend more of my time. That is one explanation for the existence of this book.

"So are you an autodidactic political economist now?" a friend asked the other day. I'm no economist at all, but the question catches something of what's happened. In 2005, with the publication of my first novel, I suddenly became a "successful" young writer: enthusiastic reviews; a brief life on the best-seller lists; translation into a dozen languages; and an option deal from a Hollywood producer with deep pockets. These very welcome developments coincided with the worst depressive episode of my adult life. I can't say what caused it, but I remember thinking of the poet Philip Larkin's line about bursting "into fulfillment's desolate attic."

Why should it have felt desolate? I'd always wanted to write novels and was now in a good position to go on doing just that. Part of the trouble seems to have been that your own fulfillment is no one else's, and therefore not even quite your own. Surely another part was that even the so-called systems-novelists I especially admired when I was younger alluded to the principal system, the economic one, more than they described or explained it: a trait of their work that had become less satisfying to me, without my knowing how to do things differently in my own. For now let it be enough to confess that I would like to live in a more fulfilling society or civilization than a self-destructive capitalist one (where, as it happens, the leading cause of death for middle-aged men in the richest country of the world is now suicide) and that these essays have been, among other things, a way of saying so. If they're assembled here in hopes of contributing to left politics, their origin probably lies in a wish to find, outside of art, some of the artistic satisfaction that comes of expressing such deep concerns that you cannot name their source.

There are other reasons why a guy with a literary background has ended up producing essays like these. For one thing, as

I've become more confident that nonspecialists can make sense of so vast a thing as capitalism, my deference to orthodox opinion has correspondingly eroded. I've been some kind of leftist for as long as I've been an adult, but not always one with complete courage of his convictions. For years I felt inhibited by the air of immense casual authority that united the mainstream press, professional economists, and prosperous male relatives when it came to the unsurpassable virtues of capitalism—a personal difficulty that might not be worth mentioning if I didn't suspect that in my timidity I had plenty of company. The 1990s weren't an ideal decade for discovering you were a socialist.

Already in the unpropitious year of 1993, with the Soviet Union freshly dissolved and amid proclamations of the liberal capitalist end of history, I'd announced to my parents, who were visiting me at college after my first year, that I was a socialist. I added that I was a *democratic* socialist who wouldn't send them to reeducation camps. They took the news with bemused indulgence. My mother has always wanted me to be happy, through socialism if necessary, while my father just asked me to define the word *reification*; besides, he is an open-minded man who not long ago told me he was enjoying the free edition of Bakunin's *God, Man and State* that I'd downloaded to a Kindle account we share. My parents in any case couldn't reproach their nineteen-year-old son with the obvious parental comeback to undergraduate avowals of socialism in a country where higher ed. costs are exorbitant: "It's our ill-gotten gains, you know, that pay for you to sit around reading about reification." This was because I'd gone to Deep

Springs College, in California, which charges no tuition or room and board: a small lesson, perhaps, in conditions favorable to intellectual freedom.

Still, for many years the national atmosphere of ideological consensus deprived me of some belief in my beliefs. Neoliberal principles were ardently proclaimed by some people I knew and shruggingly accepted by most of the rest. Where economic prosperity was lacking, excessive government deserved the blame. Maximum liberation of the market would secure the best social outcomes not only in terms of aggregate wealth but its concentration in deserving hands. Socialism of any kind was a recipe for political oppression and shoddy goods, whereas free markets could be counted on to foster democracy and other forms of consumer choice.

My respect for neoliberal doctrine, always resentful and incomplete, was a reflex all the same. It could be triggered by the flushed faces of politicians on TV or the hearty dispositions of businessmen or finance guys met in real life; it could be activated by the smooth invisible inferences drawn by newspaper journalists whenever a wave of growth swept another country adopting economic "reform," in the neutral-sounding promotional term for deregulating capital and labor markets. I armed myself against these forces with facts and counterarguments, and occasionally shouted sarcastic invective at uncles over dinner. But for years I didn't write directly about politics or economics, or imagine that I would.

The best reason for this was my desire to write fiction instead. At the age of twenty I might have considered (as I still do today) the capitalist culture industry an enemy of the sort of things I liked to read and hoped to write, but the judgment drew its strength from an even stronger desire to deal with life in the free, full way of the novelist. So when I left Deep Springs for a "real" college (its reality attested by the sums it charged), I enrolled as an English major. Besides, people at Harvard said that the economics department, headed at the time by a former advisor to the Reagan administration, had been purged of Marxists in the '70s, while in the America of the '90s it seemed that literature departments, at least, could still harbor them. (I was already a somewhat perplexed enthusiast of Fredric Jameson, a literature professor at Duke and the subject of the second essay here.) Then, too, a writer like Thoreau offered a deeper if more oblique articulation of my issues with capitalism than weekly numbers of the *Nation*. The first chapter of *Walden*—about, essentially, how to spend the windfall of your days alive—is after all called "Economy," and proposes a vision of life very different, in its spiritual pointedness and material modesty, from that of an endless series of forty-plus-hour work weeks devoted, in the end, to increasing someone else's capital. A living hero of mine like Don DeLillo could meanwhile chart the underground rivers of dread and waste flowing beneath the bright clean surfaces of capitalist prosperity, and I wanted to write novels that did something like that.

After graduation I kept writing fiction and started writing book reviews, mainly for left publications like *In These Times* and *Dissent*. My chief pastimes may have been chasing romantic love and artistic glory, with no lasting results in either department, but I took the time to harangue friends and girlfriends about entities like the Federal Reserve and the IMF and, more rarely, to join large crowds protesting a neoliberal economic summit or imperial war. Whatever motivated these actions, it wasn't hope. I believed, but uncertainly, in a better kind of economy and society, and my desire for it to come about wasn't easy to tell from despair.

In a memory from 1998 I'm sitting with a friend in a borrowed car, one Sunday evening in late spring, on a side street in lower Manhattan. A phalanx of corporate office towers stands over us as twilight drains from the air. My friend Jon Cook and I have been attending the Socialist Scholars Conference, the annual conclave later renamed the Left Forum, and are talking, naturally, about global capitalism. The mood of the memory, tinted blue by the hour, is one of mild but distinct hopelessness. One of us has just referred to the financial district around us, including the twin towers of the World Trade Center, as *the belly of the beast*, and it seems to us that from our position in the belly there isn't anything we can do to provoke the least indigestion in the beast.

At the same conference, I'd met the anarchist and scholar David Graeber (whose book *Debt: The First 5,000 Years* furnishes the subject of another essay here). Graeber struck me then, and on the half-dozen later occasions when we hung out, as a brilliant mind and fascinating talker, but by no means as the sort of person ever likely to be profiled by a major business magazine—as he was in 2011, when *Bloomberg Business Week* described his connection to a meteoric social movement called Occupy Wall Street. Throughout the '90s and deep into the past decade, the tide of events appeared to be running in a direction opposite to what I couldn't even call my hopes, as the center-left parties of wealthy countries, the electorates of the former Soviet bloc, and the central committee of the Chinese Communist Party all ratified their commitment to capitalism.

This was the ideological setting in which the narrator of my novel *Indecision*, in a drunken speech at his high school reunion, declared himself a democratic socialist. The gesture seemed both a ridiculous and necessary one for Dwight Wilmerding. His foolishness or naiveté was meant, I think, to allow him to look at the world—which could only be that of neoliberal globalization—with relatively fresh eyes, yet the book couldn't help but imply that my (anti)hero had found a politics most available, among privileged Americans during the Bush years, to the immature, clownish, and/or stoned (as well as to academics, like Dwight's sister Alice). Fiction is a form hospitable to ambiguity, and my novel must have emerged in part from my uncertainty about whether or not we American leftists were on a fool's errand, and whether the class origins of many of us didn't compromise our commitments in advance.

Even when any prospect of political deliverance seemed like a joke, capitalism at least kept me interested, and in early 2008 the novelist Chad Harbach and I formed what we called the Red/Green Reading Group. The two-man RGRG, pledged to the economic and ecological analysis of capitalism, discussed its findings every other week over beers. The first big book we tackled was *The Limits to Capital* (1981) by the Marxist geographer David Harvey (whose more recent work occasioned another of the essays). We were somewhere in the middle of Harvey's closely argued pages, which pay special attention to the role of property markets in capitalist crises, when the investment bank Bear Stearns collapsed from misbegotten investments in mortgage-backed securities. I can't say the complete financial panic that broke out six months later didn't surprise Chad and me, but we were less taken aback than, for example, Alan Greenspan, former chairman of the Federal Reserve, who admitted before a congressional hearing to being "shocked" to discover a "flaw in the model that I perceived as the critical functioning structure of how the world works." The five years since 2008 have confirmed the bafflement of many other economists in the face of a crisis more successfully anticipated by a number of Marxists outside the discipline than by all but a few of its credentialed members.

Not long before Greenspan's testimony, I'd left New York City for Buenos Aires, where I wound up living for four years. Expatriation wasn't political; I'd simply fallen for Buenos Aires on a first visit a few years earlier, maybe through some special susceptibility to the mixture of beauty and dilapidation, romanticism and cynicism, remoteness and cosmopolitanism that many visitors have tried to describe. Life in New York had in any case made too many claims on my time and money, while in Argentina at first I knew hardly a soul to tempt me away from my desk, and prices were still low enough that I could live on the proceeds of my novel much more cheaply than in New York. I was thereby relieved of the need to produce another "successful" novel in short order, and could write whatever I wanted. This turned out to be an allegorical one-act play about global warming, put up at a small theater in Buenos Aires in 2011, which seems to me the best thing I've done and which no one in the States has shown an interest in producing; a long half-finished novel currently set aside in favor of an autodidactic political treatise; some poetry best shielded from the light of day; and a number of essays for *n+1* and the *LRB*.

In Buenos Aires I lived in a long drafty apartment with thrillingly tall ceilings that I shared for a year with the writer and critic Emily Cooke, as well as with two, then three cats. (The third we adopted when she was a few ounces of flea-ridden black fur yowling at the elements during one of those Buenos Aires downpours when the skies just hemorrhage.) Then Emily went back to New York, and I discovered that to be a man living alone with three cats in an exceptionally far-away foreign country, among piles of economic tracts and drifts of printed-out articles, is to invite suspicions of craziness—though my *porteño* friends showed me the tolerance for apparent craziness which, according to them, life in their city requires.

Another result of living in Buenos Aires was to place me at a certain sharp angle to the neoliberalism that had already come to grief there. This isn't the place to rehearse recent Argentine history (which my essay "Argentinidad," published in *n+1*, discusses in the context of the country's 2010 bicentennial), except to say that during the '90s Argentina undertook textbook neoliberalizing measures which failed gradually and then, in the southern summer of 2001–02, all at once, when the country suffered perhaps the worst collapse of any sizeable economy after the Depression. Since then, Argentina has set itself apart from fellow members of the G-20 by the anti-neoliberal character of the government's rhetoric and, to a lesser extent, policies; by a rate of economic growth that was for many years the highest in Latin America; and by the emergence of a radical protest culture long before Occupy or the *indignados*. To live in Buenos Aires when I did seems to have slightly enlarged my sense of historical possibility—and that may inflect the essays here.

The oldest of them I drafted over a few hot summer days of December 2009. I, too, wondered what I was doing writing a long essay called "Full Employment." But in the English-language newspapers and magazines I was reading online, story after story cited the alarming unemployment figures in the US and elsewhere without placing them in what seemed to me their obvious historical context, namely the chronic failure of the rich countries to achieve full employment since the 1970s. I wrote "Full Employment," in other words, because the qualified people wouldn't. Economic journalists were too engrossed by the data of the moment, while academic economists were too technical in approach and arid in language to address a general audience, not to mention too bewildered, many of them, by the implosion of their ideology. The essay also gave me a chance to discuss the Marxist historian Robert Brenner, whose *Economics of Global Turbulence* (2006) concludes anticipating the financial crisis that would break out two years after the book was published.

Earlier in 2009, *GQ* magazine had asked me to profile the economist Nouriel Roubini, famous for having more clearly foreseen the crisis than any of his academic colleagues. Roubini is a man of real intelligence and learning, and there weren't many questions about macroeconomics I could pose that he hadn't already considered. An exception came when I asked his opinion of Brenner's theory of the "long down-turn" since the early '70s. Since Roubini wasn't familiar with it, I explained the argument that chronic overcapacity in manufacturing has discouraged investment in expanded industrial production, tempting available capital into finan-cial speculation instead, with an escalating series of specula-tive crises as one result. Roubini didn't have much to say at the time, but a day or two later he wrote asking to be reminded of the author and title of the book I'd mentioned—a sign both of his personal broadmindedness and the closed charac-ter of his discipline.

My career as a *marxisant* reporter for a high-end men's life-style magazine didn't last. For my next and, it turned out, final assignment, *GQ* flew me from Buenos Aires to Dubai, to report on the plummeting real estate market. Many journalists had already described (as I did too) the proliferation of chees-ily sumptuous luxury hotels and condominium towers, in stories that less often dwelled on the immigrant guest-work-ers, forbidden by law to unionize, who built the structures. I thought it might be worthwhile visiting one of Dubai's labor camps, and therefore loitered around a shopping mall parking lot in the drab slum of Al Quoz asking South Asian workers with minimal English for a glimpse of their living quarters, and mainly eliciting the sort of brisk refusal due a sex-tourist who has wandered off the beaten path. At last a friendly Nepali guy of twenty-six named Kaushi, in Dubai as a security guard, was willing to show me the room he shared with three other employees of the same firm. His roommate Karma, an ancient-looking man of thirty, was slipping on his flip-flops when I entered a room just wide enough for a person to stand between the metal bunk beds pressed to either wall. The place contained four gym lockers, a cubby for shoes, some synthetic fleece blankets, a bath towel, and a Nepali newsmagazine. It was impossible not to be struck by the fact that workers who slept four to a windowless room spent their waking hours guarding vast glass-enclosed luxury apartments most of which were going uninhabited, either for want of a buyer or because they hadn't been purchased to house people in the first place, only capital.

On the cover of the newsmagazine was a story about the Maoist rebellion in Nepal, which at the time had just ended with the restoration of democracy and the inclusion of former guerillas in the government, and in my best tones of journalistic neutrality I asked Kaushi and Karma whether they liked the Maoists or not.

"No, sir," said Karma, the ancient-looking thirty-year-old.

Handsome and confident Kaushi, however, said, "Yes, I am Maoist."

This inspired Karma to change his answer. "I am Maoist also."

"So you guys support communism?" I asked them. "You want a workers' revolution?"

"Yes, sir," said Karma, bashfully.

Kaushi—who, I noticed, never called me *sir*—wasn't shy at all about his enthusiasm for workers' revolution, and asked me if I wanted one.

"I'm definitely thinking about it." And that was how my article ended, which may or may not have influenced *GQ*'s editors to kill the piece and neglect to solicit future contributions from me.

Most of my youth went by during the end of history, which has itself now come to an end. If no serious alternative to liberal capitalism can yet be made out, surely it's also become difficult for anyone paying attention to view the present system as viable. The more substantial book I intend to be my next will sketch a different possible order. The aim is not unique; several important postcapitalist visions marked by what might be called a tough-minded utopianism (notably, in the US, *After Capitalism* by David Schweickart, and *What Then Must We Do?* by Gar Alperovitz) have appeared in the past few years alone. Yet the two decades from 1989 to 2008 were notable for their dearth of revolutionary platforms or utopian imagery, which had perhaps never been so scarce since "the left" first acquired its name during the French Revolution (thanks to the Assemblée Nationale's practice of assigning seats on the left side of its chamber to newer and often more radical delegates).

In the era of the end of history, mass political parties that might have advanced a transformative program were almost everywhere going over to neoliberalism, shedding adherents, or both. The very idea of revolutionary socialism seemed discredited by Communist terror from the Bolsheviks to the Khmer Rouge and the failure of centralized planning in the countries of the Warsaw Pact. The typical interpretation of Soviet disintegration was that Marxism stood disproved and capitalism vindicated. "Another World Is Possible," said the placards at demonstrations, and to insist on that point may have been about as much as could be done at a time when so many denied it and the left had no platform to offer, only a few stray planks.

Over the past five years or so, a different era has begun. For more and more people, global capitalism is losing or has already lost its air of careless munificence, strewing its blessings generously if unevenly across the world, as well as that claim to final historical inevitability that could always be made when other justifications failed. It's in light of this change that the next-to-last essay here argues, against Slavoj Žižek and others, that the left needs to supplement its anticapitalism with a basic conception of another order, a sort of minimum utopian program (no doubt to be continually elaborated and revised by societies in a position to enact it). Capitalism is after all not the worst conceivable form of economic organization; the point is to ask whether something better and less ecologically fatal may succeed it, and what that might be.

This book only hints at an answer. Its main burden is to introduce a half-dozen bodies of contemporary thought by writers who have been more concerned to diagnose the economic or cultural condition of capitalism than to imagine a successor. Their emphasis has not been misplaced. The past and present are available to study as the future can't be; more than this, it was only natural for left intellectuals in recent decades to devote their energies not to political strategy, revolutionary programs, or utopian devisings, but to the analysis of this or that feature of capitalism. Marxism had first to survive before it could recover a more constructive role. (Anarchism, the fraternal rival accompanying revolutionary socialism through modern history, emerged from the past two decades in better political shape: less theoretically developed than Marxism and never used as a warrant for party dictatorships, it had, among other attractions, less explaining to do before it could move on to new tasks.)

The past few years have seen a revival of Marxist thought, which might loosely be defined as the collective effort to contemplate capitalism as a whole or, in the traditional idiom, a totality, from the standpoint of a politics of its transcendence. (One sign of this in the US has been the birth of *Jacobin* magazine, under whose imprimatur this collection appears: a publication addressed to a general audience most of whose contributors would probably accept the label "Marxist.") The recovery of Marxism, still very new and incomplete, was already underway before 2008, as Cold War taboos faded and global capitalism manifested its dominance in many of the smallest as well as the largest features of contemporary life. Any regime on such a scale may be, for some of its subjects, so pervasive as to become invisible, but will compel others to dissent. Since 2008, generalized crisis has exposed to wider view the shortcomings of mainstream economics and other non-Marxist varieties of social thought, much as the historian

Perry Anderson foresaw in 1992. Pointing out that intellectual approaches to society once considered outmoded had
recently acquired new life (in renovated forms of structural-
ism, evolutionism, functionalism, and existentialism),
Anderson predicted that

> the future of Marxism is unlikely to be different. Its most
> powerful intellectual challengers . . . share a blind side
> whose importance is constantly increasing. They have
> little, if anything, to say about the dynamics of the capital-
> ist economy that now rules without rival over the fate of
> the earth. Here the normative theory which has accompa-
> nied its triumph is equally—indeed avowedly—bereft:
> the Hayekian synthesis, for all its other strengths, disclaim-
> ing systematic explanations of the paths of long-term
> growth or structural crisis. The come-back of historical
> materialism will probably be on this terrain.

The economic doctrine, inspired by Friedrich von Hayek,
to which Anderson referred is today more often called neoliberalism, as is the accompanying politics. (Not by its practitioners, however: like a dog unaware of its name, a political
regime answering to no designation can better elude control
by its supposed master, the citizenry, than one which turns its
head when called.) The present economic crisis is one that
neoliberal economists cannot explain, and that even their
Keynesian colleagues can account for only incompletely. It is
also a crisis that neoliberal politicians—whether free-market
boosters of the right, technocrats of the center, or

muddlers-through of the former left—cannot credibly propose to resolve. Their delinquency in the face of history has had many dire effects; a rare auspicious one has been to tempt people who knew little about Marxism beyond its reputation as debunked economics and totalitarian politics to look into the matter for themselves.

More important than intellectual debates is a generational shift underway. Global capitalism or neoliberalism under US hegemony or just the way things are going: call it whatever you like, it has inflicted economic insecurity and ecological anxiety on the young in particular. They emerge today from their schooling onto job markets reluctant to accommodate them at all, let alone on stable or generous terms, and they will bear the consequences of planetary ecological disorder in proportion to the years lying ahead of them. In any genuine renaissance of Marxist thought and culture, it will probably be decisive that capitalism has forfeited the allegiance of many people who are today under thirty.

In the meantime Marxism surely remains a bogeyman or forbidding mystery to far more people than not. Whether this changes counts for more than whether the name *Marxism* is retained. The name pays homage to a brilliant, admirable, flawed man of the nineteenth century: an excellent and entertaining father, a devoted if not entirely faithful husband, a tremendously hard worker who was also a serious procrastinator, and a generous personality prone to a terrible anger that can mar his writing too. Is this well-merited tribute, not only to Marx himself but to the best of his intellectual and political heirs, a price worth paying for the connotations

Marxism acquired during the twentieth century? If so, let the word thrive along with the thing itself; if not, it can fall away.

Marxism under whatever name can only serve present needs as a set of questions, not a battery of ready answers. These include questions about the development of capitalism, from its genesis to the present day; about the role of class struggle in historical change; about the relationship between social classes and government; about how culture reflects—or can't help reflecting—economic conditions; and about how a climate of opinion or "hegemony" achieves the consent of exploited people.

Other questions are more prospective in nature. How can the left build a hegemony of its own, to both prefigure and prepare a new society? What factors are likely to bring about the end, gradual or sudden, of capitalism? How should a postcapitalist society be run to ensure the dissolution of social classes as opposed to domination by any one class? How would ownership and control of productive resources be shared in the society we want? How far are markets compatible with such changes? What way of organizing social reproduction might be most satisfying to us both while we are working and while we are not? A list like this is far from exhaustive, nor do the questions themselves admit of final answers. Even so, better or worse answers can be given, and Marxists will usually have the best answers to questions that often they alone are willing to pose. None of which is to deny that historical materialism has paid too little attention to issues—of social scale and complexity, of relations between the sexes, of the logic of war or nationalism or ecology or technology—that ought to be fundamental to it. Far from having all the answers, it hasn't even had all the questions. Still, the commitment of Marxism to contemplating capitalism in its entirety, in the light of earlier modes of production and those which may lie ahead, gives it a capacity to confront social matters in their interrelationship—including their ostensible disconnection—that no other way of thinking can claim.

"Communism is the riddle to history solved," the young Marx wrote, a proposition he did not repeat. The same can't be said of Marxism, which is better understood as an attempt to formulate the riddle of history with due fullness, complexity, and urgency. The stakes of this effort, as they appear to me, are summarized in the title to this otherwise modest and retrospective book: *Utopia or Bust*.

1

David Harvey: Crisis Theory

The deepest economic crisis in eighty years prompted a shallow revival of Marxism. During the panicky period between the failure of Lehman Brothers in September 2008 and the official end of the American recession in the summer of 2009, several mainstream journals, displaying a less than sincere mixture of broadmindedness and chagrin, hailed Marx as a neglected seer of capitalist crisis. The trend-spotting *Foreign Policy* led the way, with a cover story on Marx, for its Next Big Thing issue, enticing readers with a promise of the star treatment: "Lights. Camera. Action. *Das Kapital.* Now."

Though written by a socialist, Leo Panitch, the piece was typical of the general approach to Marx and Marxism. It bowed at a distance to the prophet of capitalism's ever "more extensive and exhaustive crises," and restated several basic articles of his thought: capitalism is inherently unstable; political activism is indispensable; and revolution offers the ultimate prize. This can't have done much more than jog memories of *The Communist Manifesto*, the only one of Marx's works cited by Panitch. The *Manifesto* remains an incandescent pamphlet, but the elements of a Marxian crisis theory, one never fully articulated by Marx himself, lie elsewhere, scattered throughout *Theories of Surplus Value*, the *Grundrisse*, and above all the posthumous second and third volumes of *Capital*. Marx's brilliant and somewhat contradictory comments on the subject bring to mind Cioran's remark "Works die; fragments, not having lived, can no longer die." Such seeds sowed one of the most fertile fields in Marxist economics. Over recent decades, the landmarks of Marxian economic thinking include Ernest Mandel's *Late Capitalism* (1972), David Harvey's *Limits to Capital* (1982), Giovanni Arrighi's *Long Twentieth Century* (1994), and Robert Brenner's *Economics of Global Turbulence* (2006), all expressly concerned with the grinding tectonics and punctual quakes of capitalist crisis. Yet little trace of this literature, by Marx or his successors, has surfaced even among the more open-minded practitioners of what might be called the bourgeois theorization of the current crisis.

The term *bourgeois* will seem apt enough if we note that a recent and distinguished addition to the long shelf of books on the crisis, Nouriel Roubini's *Crisis Economics*, summons as its audience not only "financial professionals," "corporate executives" and "students in business, economics and finance," but also—exhausting the list—"ordinary investors." No one, in other words, who is unmotivated by gain. Maybe it's to be expected, then, that the Marx celebrated by Roubini and his coauthor Stephen Mihm, in a résumé of earlier theorists of crisis, appears as a mere herald of continual disruption rather than as an economist who located at the heart of such crises the existence of bourgeois society as such, or the social cleavage between profit-seekers (financial professionals etc.) and wage-earners: the fatal schism, in other words, between capital and labor. Roubini goes no further than to quote the same ringing lines of the *Manifesto* that appear in *Foreign Policy*. Here again is the resemblance of capitalism to "the sorcerer who is no longer able to control the powers of the nether world whom he has called up by his spells." Credited with the alarming but vague insight that "Capitalism *is* crisis," Marx then departs the scene.

To date, a revived Keynesianism has formed a left boundary of economic debate in the press at large. Only specialized socialist journals have undertaken to diagnose capitalism's latest distemper in explicitly or implicitly Marxian terms. As for books on the crisis, until recently the jostling crowd of English-language titles included no Marxist study, the exception to this rule, John Bellamy Foster and Fred Magdoff's *Great Financial Crisis*, having been bolted together out of editorials from one of those socialist journals, the *Monthly Review*. Not until now, with David Harvey's *The Enigma of Capital: And the Crises of Capitalism* have we had a book-length example of Marxian crisis theory addressed to the current situation.*

Few writers could be better qualified than Harvey to test the continuing validity of a Marxian approach to crisis, a situation he helpfully defines—dictionaries of economics tend to

---

* This was to miss *Zombie Capitalism* (2009) by Chris Harman, the late British Trotskyist. Harman integrates Marxian theory with a history of capitalist crises from the nineteenth century to that of 2008, which erupted after he had started his book, and is a particularly lucid exponent of the theory of the falling rate of profit.

lack any entry for the word—as "surplus capital and surplus labor existing side by side with seemingly no way to put them back together." (This is at once reminiscent of Keynes's "underemployment equilibrium" and of the news in the daily papers: in the US, corporations are sitting on almost two trillion dollars in cash while unemployment hovers just below 10 percent.) Harvey, who was born in Kent, England, is the author of the monumental *Limits to Capital*—a thoroughgoing critique, synthesis, and extension of the several varieties of crisis theory underwritten by Marx's thought—and has been teaching courses on Marx, mainly in the States, for nearly four decades. His lectures on Volume I of *Capital*, available online, have become part of the self-education of many young leftists, and now supply the framework for his useful *Companion to Marx's Capital*. (I sat in on his lectures at the City University of New York in the fall of 2007; a good Marxist, Harvey made no effort to find out whether any of us—too many for the available chairs—had registered and paid for the class.)

Since the publication of *The Limits to Capital* in the second year of the Reagan administration and at the dawn of what has come to be known as the financialization of the world economy, the dual movement of Harvey's career has been to return time and again to Marx as a teacher, and to extend his own ideas into new and more empirical territory. The most substantial of his recent books, *Paris, Capital of Modernity* (2003), described the city's forcible modernization by Baron Haussmann as a solution to structural crisis —"The problem in 1851 was to absorb the surpluses of capital and labor power"—and situated this urban transformation within the renovation of Parisian society and culture it induced. Harvey's other postmillennial volumes, *The New Imperialism* (also 2003), *A Brief History of Neoliberalism* (2005), and now *The Enigma of Capital*, amount to a trilogy of self-popularization and historical illustration, taking current events as a proving ground for what Harvey has called, referring to *The Limits to Capital*, "a reasonably good approximation to a general theory of capital accumulation in space and time."

The mention of space is considered. Harvey received his doctorate in geography rather than economics or history—his first, non-Marxist book was taken up with differing representations of space—and the whole thrust of his subsequent work, alert to the unevenness of capitalist development across neighborhoods, regions, and nation-states, has been to give a more variegated spatial texture to the historical materialism he would prefer to call "historical-geographical materialism." In a sense, the emphasis confirms Harvey's classicism. Marx himself somewhat curiously concluded the first volume of *Capital*—a book otherwise essentially concerned with local transactions between capital and labor, illustrated mostly from the English experience—with a chapter discussing the "primitive accumulation" of land and mineral wealth attendant on the European sacking of the Americas. In the same way, Rosa Luxemburg, Marx's first great legatee in the theory of crisis, insisted in *The Accumulation of Capital* (1913) that imperial expansion across space must accompany capital accumulation over time. Without the prizing open of new markets in the colonies, she argued, metropolitan capitalism would be unable to dispose profitably of its glut of commodities, and crises of overproduction doom the system.

It's not, however, until the last third of *The Limits to Capital* that the spatial implications of Harvey's project loom into view. The book starts as a patient philological reconstruction, from Marx's stray comments, of a Marxian theory of crisis. The method is fittingly cumulative as, from chapter to chapter, in lucid, mostly unadorned prose, Harvey adds new features to a simple model of the "overaccumulation of capital." And overaccumulation remains in his later work—including *The Enigma of Capital*—the fount of all crisis . The term may seem paradoxical: what could it mean for capital to overaccumulate, when the entire spirit of the system is, as Marx wrote, "accumulation for accumulation's sake"? How could capitalism acquire too much of what it regards as the sole good thing?

Overaccumulated capital can be defined as capital unable to realize the expected rate of profit. Whether in the form of money, physical plant, commodities for sale, or labor power (the latter being, in Marx's terms, mere "variable capital"), it can only be invested, utilized, sold or hired, as the case may be, with reduced profitability or at a loss. Overaccumulation will then be variously reflected in money hoarded or gambled rather than invested; in underused factories or vacant storefronts; in half-finished goods or unsold inventories; and in idle workers, even as the need for all these things goes unmet. In such cases, the most basic of the contradictions Marx discovered in capitalism—between use value and exchange value—reasserts itself. For at times of crisis, it's not that too much wealth exists to make use of—in fact, "too little is produced to decently and humanely satisfy the wants of the great mass"—but that "too many means of labor and necessities of life are produced" to serve "as means for the exploitation of laborers at a certain rate of profit." A portion of the overaccumulated capital will then be devalued, until what survives can seek a satisfactory profitability again. Thus asset prices plunge, firms go bankrupt, physical inventories languish, and wages are reduced, though this devaluation is no more equally divided among the respective social groups (rentiers, industrialists, merchants, laborers) than prosperity was during the good times.

On Harvey's account, standard in this respect, the risk of overaccumulation is intrinsic to the capitalist pursuit of "surplus value." The temptation is to say that surplus value is merely Marx's name for profit, but this would be to assume success where there is only speculation: surplus value (in commodities) can be realized as a profit (in money) only in the event of a sale, and this is the rub. A capitalist, in order to produce, must purchase both means of production (Marx's "constant capital") and wage-labor (or "variable capital"). After this outlay—C+V in Marx's formulation—the capitalist naturally hopes to possess a commodity capable of being sold for more than was spent on its production. The difference between cost of production and price at sale permits the realization of surplus value. The production of any commodity, as well as the "expanded reproduction" of the system itself, can thus be described by the further formula C+V+S: to a quantity of constant capital, or means of production, has been added a quantity of variable capital, or labor power, with a bonus of surplus value contained in the finished commodity.

The trouble is already there to see. Imagine an economy consisting of a single firm which has bought means of production and labor power for a total of $100, in order to produce a mass of commodities it intends to sell for $110, i.e. at a profit of 10 percent. The problem is that the firm's suppliers of constant and variable capital are also its only potential customers. Even if the would-be buyers pool their funds, they have only their $100 to spend, and no more. Production of the total supply of commodities exceeds the monetarily effective demand in the system. As Harvey explains in *The Limits to Capital*, effective demand "is at any one point equal to C+V, whereas the value of the total output is C+V+S. Under conditions of equilibrium, this still leaves us with the problem of where the demand for S, the surplus value produced but not yet realized through exchange, comes from." An extra $10 in value must be found somewhere, to be exchanged with the firm if it is to realize its desired profit.

In this stylized scheme, with the entire capitalist economy figured as a single firm, the supplementary value can be produced only by the same firm and only in the future. The full cash value of today's product can therefore be realized only with the assistance of money advanced against commodity values yet to be produced. "The surplus value created at one point requires the creation of surplus value at another point," as Marx put it in the *Grundrisse*. How are these points, separated in space and time, to be linked? In a word, through the credit system, which involves "the creation of what Marx calls 'fictitious capital'—money that is thrown into circulation as capital without any material basis in commodities or productive activity." Money values backed by tomorrow's as yet unproduced goods and services, to be exchanged against those already produced today: this is credit or bank money, an anticipation of future value without which the creation of present value stalls. Realization (or the transformation of surplus value into its money equivalent, as profit) thus depends on the "fictitious."

Harvey is not adding to Marx here: his achievement is to piece a heap of fragments into a coherent mosaic. And for his reconstructed Marx, the end of capitalism—or at least its latest stage, of globally integrated finance—lies in its beginning. What is sometimes called the system's GOD imperative, for Grow Or Die, entails from the outset the development of finance as the earnest of future production. Finance and production, production and finance, can then chase each other's tail until together they have covered the entire world (or exhausted the tolerance of the working class). Marx proposed that "the tendency to create the world market is directly given in the concept of capital itself," and Harvey glosses the idea: "The necessary geographical expansion of capitalism is . . . to be interpreted as capital in search for surplus value. The penetration of capitalist relations into all sectors of the economy, the mobilization of various 'latent' sources of labor power (women and children, for example), have a similar basis." Hence both the involution and the imperialism of capital, commodifying the most intimate of

formerly uncommodified practices (education, food prepara-
tion, courtship) as well as sweeping formerly non-capitalist
regions (China and Eastern Europe) into the global market.

Marxist economic writing at its best praises the system it
comes to bury in more dazzling terms than more apologetic
accounts ever achieve, and Harvey's sardonic paean to "the
immense potential power that resides within the credit
system" finds him at his most eloquent. For if it at first
appeared from a logical point of view that capitalism must
immediately founder in a crisis of overproduction and underconsumption it now appears that this problem enjoys a solution. Consider, Harvey suggests, "the relation between
production and consumption":

> A proper allocation of credit can ensure a quantitative
> balance between them. The gap between purchases and
> sales . . . can be bridged, and production can be harmo-
> nized with consumption to ensure balanced accumulation.
> Any increase in the flow of credit to housing construction,
> for example, is of little avail today without a parallel
> increase in the flow of mortgage finance to facilitate hous-
> ing purchases. Credit can be used to accelerate production
> and consumption simultaneously.

In the aftermath of the greatest housing bust in history, from
Phoenix to Dublin to Dubai, that should sound an ominous note.
Harvey goes on: "All links in the realization process of capital
bar one can be brought under the control of the credit system.
The single exception is of the greatest importance." Credit can

coordinate the flow of economic value, but can't create it ex nihilo: "There is no substitute for the actual transformation of nature through the concrete production of use values."

In the case of real estate, it might happen—as it has—that more building and selling of houses has been financed than can actually be paid for with income deriving, in the last instance, from production. So the credit system that had seemed to insure against one kind of overaccumulation (of commodity capital) by advancing money against future production now seems to have fostered another kind of over-accumulation (of fictitious capital) by promising more production than has occurred. More housing has been created than builders can sell at a profit; more mortgage debt has been issued than can be repaid, through wage income, to ensure the lenders' profit; homeowners who took out loans against the rising value of their property find that prices are instead plummeting; and with the collapse of the housing sector more money capital now lies in the hands of its owners than they can see a way to invest profitably.

"The onset of a crisis is usually triggered by a spectacular failure which shakes confidence in fictitious forms of capital," Harvey writes, and everyone knows what happens next. The flow of credit, at one moment lavished on all comers with the flimsiest pretext of repayment, at the next more or less dries up. In the resulting conditions of uncertainty, those without ready cash, forced to cough it up anyway, can be pushed into fire-sales of their assets, while those who do have cash prefer to save rather than spend it, so that the economy as a whole sinks toward stagnation. So far, so familiar. But what explains the special liability of capitalism to crises of disappointed speculation? And why should real estate so often be their privileged object?

"Such speculative fevers are not necessarily to be interpreted as direct manifestations of disequilibrium in production," Harvey says. "They can and do occur on their own account." Yet "overaccumulation creates conditions ripe for such speculative fevers so that a concatenation of the latter almost invariably signals the existence of the former." If capital has been overaccumulated, this means by definition that it can't easily find a profitable outlet in increased production. The resulting temptation, Harvey suggests, with his emphasis on finance, will be for capital to sidestep production altogether and attempt to increase itself through the multiplication of paper (or digital) assets alone. The question that goes all but unasked in the more respectable literature on the crisis is why the opportunities for profitable investment looked so scarce in the first place.

If capitalist crises are crises of profitability, Marxian theory ascribes diminished opportunities for profit to one of three underlying conditions. First, a profit squeeze may be induced by the excessive wage bill of the working class, so that capitalists lack enough income to invest in new production on a scale compatible with growth. This line of thought takes inspiration from Marx's remark that wages are never higher than on the eve of a crash, and enjoyed a heyday of plausibility in the early 1970s, a bygone era of labor militancy, near full employment, and high inflation, allegedly spurred by the so-called wage-price spiral. Robert Brenner disputes, however, that a profit squeeze imposed by labor truly afflicted the early 1970s, and doubts whether, given the superior mobility of capital over labor, such a profit squeeze could ever take hold over the long run; capital would simply relocate to more docile markets. At any rate, what Brenner calls the Full Employment Profit Squeeze thesis hardly appears to caption the current picture of high unemployment and stagnant real wages across the developed world.

A second condition is the tendency of the rate of profit to fall as a result of the "rising organic composition of capital," or in other words the penchant, given increased technological and organizational efficiency, for using relatively less labor than capital in production. Since profitability reflects the "rate of exploitation"—or the ratio of the surplus value produced by the worker to the wages he receives—using less labor relative to capital diminishes profitability, unless capital goods become cheaper or exploitation is ramped up. This problem too can be solved, at least in principle: the capital/labor ratio can simply be rejiggered by deploying more labor relative to capital. Indeed, something like this seems to have occurred on the grandest scale in recent decades, through the rough doubling of the amount of labor available to capital with the proletarianization of huge populations in Eastern Europe and Asia. The effect, on one estimate, has been to reduce the global capital/labor ratio by 55–60 percent.

Finally, and most plausibly today, theories of "underconsumption" argue that capitalism slips toward crisis because, by resisting wage growth, it deprives itself of the market, expanded by wage growth, it would need in order to profitably employ its swelling quantities of capital. Marx, in Volume II of *Capital*, is to the point: "Contradiction in the capitalist mode of production: the laborers as buyers of commodities are important for the market. But as sellers of their own commodity—labor power—capitalist society tends to keep them down to the minimum price." Of course "a sufficient prodigality of the capitalist class," as Marx called it, could in principle maintain effective demand at a level consistent with the steady expansion of the system, by substituting luxury consumption for the satisfaction of the population at large.* But this solution was never likely, since as Keynes observed, "when our income increases our consumption increases also, but not by so much. The key to our practical problem is to be found in this psychological law." The worldwide defeat of labor since the 1980s, leading the wage share of GDP to fall throughout the capitalist core, along with the persistent inability of the higher reaches of the capitalist class, in spite of best efforts, to attain a level of expenditure proportionate to their wealth, makes an underconsumptionist analysis of the current crisis an appealing one, and suggests a possible convergence of Keynesian and Marxian views.

Marxists tend to battle each other, often in the heroic footnotes native to the tradition, over the merits or defects of these differing explanations of crisis. Harvey's own approach is

---

* In his 1865 lecture on "Value, Price and Profit," Marx illustrated luxury consumption as money "wasted on flunkeys, horses, cats and so forth." It is some measure of progress that the general population can now afford to keep cats.

catholic, all-encompassing. For him, the various strands of crisis theory represent, but don't exhaust, possible departures from a path of balanced growth in finance and production. What unites the strands is the fundamental antagonism between capital and labor, with their opposing pursuits of profits and wages. If there exists a theoretical possibility of attaining an ideal proportion, from the standpoint of balanced growth, between the amount of total social income to be reinvested in production and the amount to be spent on consumption, and if at the same time the credit system could serve to maintain this ratio of profits to wages in perpetuity, the antagonistic nature of class society nevertheless prevents such a balance from being struck except occasionally and by accident, to be immediately upset by any advantage gained by labor or, more likely, by capital.

So, as *The Limits to Capital* implies without quite stating, the special allure and danger of an elaborate credit system lie in its relationship to class society. If more capital has been accumulated than can be realized as a profit through exchange, owing perhaps to "the poverty and restricted consumption of the masses" that Marx at one point declared "the ultimate reason for all real crises," this condition can be temporarily concealed, and its consequences postponed, by the confection of fictitious values in excess of any real values on the verge of production. In this way, growth and profitability in the financial system can substitute for the impaired growth and profitability of the class-ridden system of actual production. By adding overfinancialization, as it were, to his model of overaccumulation, Harvey means to show how an initial contradiction between production and realization later "becomes, via the agency of the credit system, an outright antagonism" between the financial system of fictitious values and its monetary base, founded on commodity values. This antagonism then "forms the rock on which accumulation ultimately founders." In social terms, this will take the form of a contest between creditors and debtors over who is to suffer more devaluation.

The real originality of *The Limits to Capital*, however, is to add a new geographical dimension to crisis formation. Harvey goes about this via a theory of rent. One effect of the approach is to suggest why property speculation—with its value ultimately tied up in potential rental income—should be such a familiar capitalist perversion (in the psychoanalytic sense of overinvestment in one kind of object). Another is to convert an apparent embarrassment for Marxian theory into a show of strength. The would-be embarrassment lies in the evident difficulty of reconciling a labor theory of value with the price of unimproved land, given that land is obviously not a product of human labor. Harvey's bold and ingenious solution is to propose that, under capitalism, ground rent—or the proportion of property value attributable to mere location, rather than to anything built or cultivated on the land—becomes a "pure financial asset." Ground rent, in other words, is a form of fictitious capital, or value created in anticipation of future commodity production: "Like all such forms of fictitious capital, what is traded is a claim on future revenues, which means a claim on future profits from the use of the land or, more directly, a claim on future labor."

From the need to realize ground rent stems capitalism's whole geography of anxious anticipation. Capital overaccumulated in one place can flow to another which appears to boast better ultimate prospects of profit. Rising land values will shunt capital to new locations, at the same time that the resulting increase in rental costs compels a matching expansion of production, with its accompanying physical and social infrastructure. The relationship between credit and commodities is in this way translated into spatial terms as an uneasy rapport between one kind of capital, highly mobile or liquid, and another kind—"fixed capital embedded in the land"—defined by its very inertness. Here, in the latent conflict between migratory finance capital and helplessly stationary complexes of fixed capital, including not only factories and office buildings but roads, houses, schools, and so on, Harvey has found a contradiction of capitalism overlooked by Marx and his heirs.

The contradiction may look at first like a brilliant solution to the problem of overaccumulation. Overaccumulated capital, whether originating as income from production or as the bank overdrafts that unleash fictitious values, can put off any immediate crisis of profitability by being drawn off into long-term infrastructural projects, in an operation Harvey calls a "spatio-temporal fix." Examples on a grand scale would be the British boom in railway construction of the 1820s, the Second Empire modernization of Paris, the suburbanization of the US after World War II, and the recent international pullulation of commercial and residential towers. In each case, a vast quantity of capital, faced with the question of profitability, could as it were postpone the answer to a remote date, since investments in infrastructure promise such delayed returns. Meanwhile, transformed spatial arrangements swap old trades for new ones—Harvey notes that Haussmann's Paris witnessed the extinction of the water-carrier and the advent of the electrician—or rejuvenate existing industries, like the postwar car manufacturers in the US.

Inevitably, the risk is that a given territory, as a complex of fixed capital, comes to prosper thanks to a stream of finance that one day flows elsewhere. A devaluation of the abandoned land along with its "overaccumulated" workers, industries, and infrastructure will ensue. This harsh sequel to the spatial fix Harvey calls a "switching crisis," and in something like the climax of *The Limits to Capital*, he writes:

> The more the forces of geographical inertia prevail, the deeper will the aggregate crises of capitalism become and the more savage will switching crises have to be to restore the disturbed equilibrium. Local alliances will have to be dramatically reorganized (the rise of Fascism being the most horrible example), technological mixes suddenly altered (incurring massive devaluation of old plant), physical and social infrastructures totally reconstituted (often through a crisis in state expenditures) and the space economy of capitalist production, distribution and consumption totally transformed. The cost of devaluation to both individual capitalists and laborers becomes substantial. Capitalism reaps the savage harvest of its own internal contradictions.

In *The Enigma of Capital* Harvey observes these contradictions sharpening over time, as finance capital becomes ever more mobile while beds of infrastructure grow increasingly Procrustean: "The disjunction of the quest for hypermobility and an increasingly sclerotic built environment (think of the huge amount of fixed capital embedded in Tokyo or New York City) becomes ever more dramatic."

So what then are the "limits to capital"? Harvey's answer, disappointing as it is honest, is that a system bent on overaccumulation will not collapse of its own top-heaviness. Should the world market fail to generate the ever-increasing surpluses that form its only rationale, it can always enlarge its borders and appropriate new wealth through what Marx called primitive accumulation and what Harvey proposes to call "accumulation by dispossession," given that the process hardly ceased when the English peasantry was cleared off the land or the Incan Empire looted for its silver. The incorporation into the capitalist domain of noncapitalist territories and populations, the privatization of public or commonly owned assets, including land, and so on, down to the commodification of indigenous art-forms and the patenting of seeds, offer instances of the accumulation by dispossession that has accompanied capitalism since its inception. This field for gain would be exhausted only with universal commodification, when "every person in every nook and cranny of the world is caught within the orbit of capital." Even then, the continuous "restructuring of the space economy of capitalism on a global scale still holds out the prospect for a restoration of equilibrium through a reorganization of the regional parts." Spatial fixes and switching crises might succeed one another endlessly, in great floods and droughts of capital. Devaluation, being "always on a particular route or at a particular place," might serially scourge the earth even as capital in general, loyal to no country, remained free to pursue its own advantage.

The real test of Harvey's 1982 theory of crisis is how well it serves in the face of the thing itself. *The Enigma of Capital* can be read as an effort to meet the challenge. Naturally, its success or failure depends on whether it can offer a more comprehensive and persuasive account than rival theories. On the score of comprehensiveness there can be little doubt that Harvey's work and that of other Marxists goes beyond the alternatives. "The idea that the crisis had systemic origins is scarcely mooted in the mainstream media," Harvey writes, and that might be extended to include even the trenchant work of the neo-Keynesians. The crisis, after all, is that of a capitalist system, and no account of it, however searching, can be truly systematic if it neglects to consider property relations: that is, the preponderant ownership of capital by one class, and of little or nothing but its labor power by another.

Paul Krugman, discussing Roubini's book in the *New York Review of Books*, agreed with him that what Ben Bernanke called the "global savings glut" lay at the heart of the crisis, behind the proximate follies of deregulation, mortgage-securitization, excessive leverage and so on. Originating in the current account surpluses of net-exporting countries such as Germany, Japan, and China, this great tide of money flooded markets in the US and Western Europe, and floated property and asset values unsustainably. Why was so much capital so badly misallocated? In the *London Review of Books* (April 22, 2010), Joseph Stiglitz observed that the savings glut "could equally well be described as an 'investment dearth,' " reflecting a scarcity of attractive investment opportunities. Stiglitz suggests that global warming mitigation or poverty reduction offers new "opportunities for investments with high social returns."

The neo-Keynesians' "savings glut" can readily be seen as a case of what a more radical tradition calls overaccumulated capital. But it is the broader and more systematic Marxist perspective that ultimately and properly contains Keynesianism within it, and a crude Marxist catechism may be in order. Where does an excess of savings come from? From unpaid labor—for example, that of Chinese or German workers. And why would such funds inflate asset bubbles rather than create useful investment? Because capital pursues not "high social returns," but high private returns. And why should these have proved difficult to achieve, except by financial shell-games? Keynesians complain of an insufficiency of aggregate demand, restraining investment. The Marxist will simply add that this bespeaks inadequate wages, in the index of a class struggle going the way of owners rather than workers.

In *The Enigma of Capital*, Harvey coincides with other Marxists in locating the origins of the present crisis in the troubles of the 1970s, when the so-called Golden Age of capitalism following World War II—blessed with high rates of profitability, productivity, wage growth, and expansion of output—gave way to what Brenner called "the long downturn" after 1973. Brenner argued in *The Economics of Global Turbulence* that this long downturn, with deeper recessions and weaker expansions across every business cycle, reflects chronic overcapacity—another variety of overaccumulation—in international manufacturing, a condition brought about by the maturation of Japanese and German industry by the end of the 1960s, and later compounded by the industrialization of East Asia. As competition to supply export markets increased faster than those markets expanded, the price of international tradeables naturally fell, reducing both the profits of manufacturers and the wages paid to workers. Such impaired profitability moreover discouraged further investment in production, so that finance capital turned increasingly to speculation in asset values. Yet this view, however formidably presented, doesn't appear to have won general assent. Harvey, content to follow Brenner elsewhere, inclines towards a more conventional profit-squeeze explanation of the crisis of the early 1970s.

About the sequel to that crisis there is less dispute. Whether or not high wages had undermined profitability, a subsequent effort to curb wages, carried out at gunpoint in the Southern Cone in the mid-1970s, and achieved by ballot under Thatcher and Reagan before spreading to other wealthy countries, eventually resulted in a systemic shortage of demand. In this way, capital's victory over labor set the stage for a later reversal. In *The Enigma of Capital*, Harvey charts the dialectical switch in the blunt style he now favors:

Labor availability is no problem now for capital, and it has not been for the last twenty-five years. But disempowered labor means low wages, and impoverished workers do not constitute a vibrant market. Persistent wage repression therefore poses the problem of lack of demand for the expanding output of capitalist corporations. One barrier to capital accumulation—the labor question—is overcome at the expense of creating another—lack of a market. So how could this second barrier be circumvented?

The lack of demand was of course appeased by recourse to fictitious capital: "The gap between what labor was earning and what it could spend was covered by the rise of the credit card industry and increasing indebtedness." It was not only consumers who indentured themselves. As Bellamy Foster and Magdoff point out in *The Great Financial Crisis*, total US debt, owed by government, corporations, and individuals, equaled approximately 125 percent of American GDP during the 1970s. By the mid-1980s the proportion had increased to two to one, and by 2005 stood at almost three and a half to one. Much of the cheap credit, originating in East Asia and flowing through the Federal Reserve, came to promote a property bubble of historic dimensions. "The demand problem," Harvey writes, "was temporarily bridged with respect to housing by debt-financing the developers as well as the buyers. The financial institutions collectively controlled both the supply of, and demand for, housing!"

It can't be said that Harvey comes late to recognizing the housing bubble's absurdity. In *The New Imperialism*, from

2003, he recapitulated his theory of the spatial fix, and warned that while some spatial fixes ultimately relieve crises through the elaboration of new physical and social infrastructure, others merely buy time. After listing several of the more spectacular property-market collapses of the long downturn (worldwide in 1973–75; Japanese in 1990; Thai and Indonesian in 1997), Harvey added that

> the most important prop to the US and British economies after the onset of general recession in all other sectors from mid-2001 onwards was the continued speculative vigor in the property and housing markets and construction. In a curious backwash effect, we find that some 20 percent of GDP growth in the United States in 2002 was attributable to consumers refinancing their mortgage debt on the inflated values of their housing and using the extra money they gained for immediate consumption (in effect, mopping up overaccumulating capital in the primary circuit). British consumers borrowed $19 billion in the third quarter of 2002 alone against the value of their mortgages to finance consumption. What happens if and when this property bubble bursts is a matter for serious concern.

Not only Americans and Britons but the Irish, Spanish, and Emiratis live today among the ruins of a broken spatial fix.

What, if any, switching crisis does this presage? To keep things simple, imagine the world economy of recent years as consisting of two capitalist countries—represented by the

US and China—in both of which the working class, employed or unemployed, received too little of the total product for capital not to overaccumulate and risk massive devaluation. Chinese workers, deprived by wage repression and social insecurity (such as lack of health insurance) of the opportunity to consume much of their own output, saw the wealth accumulated through their labor go, in the form of their own savings and the income of their bosses, towards the construction of new productive capacity in their own country and a property boom in the other country. Both the new factories at home, turning out exports for the US, and the deliriously appreciating houses abroad rested on the premise of continuously rising American incomes. But among Americans, wage growth had ceased and household incomes could no longer be supplemented by the mass entry of women into the workforce, something already accomplished. The issuance and securitization of debt alone could substitute for present income. In the end, so much fictitious capital could not be redeemed. Whatever the destination of future Chinese savings gluts, they are unlikely to sponsor American consumption in the same way.

In his final book, *Adam Smith in Beijing* (2007), the late Giovanni Arrighi expanded on Harvey's concepts of the spatial fix and the switching crisis to survey half a millennium of capitalist development and to peer into a new, perhaps Chinese century. In Arrighi's scheme of capitalist history, there have been four "systemic cycles of accumulation," each lasting roughly a century and each organized on a larger scale than the one before, with a new polity at the center: a

Genoese-Iberian cycle; a Dutch cycle; a British cycle; and an American one. A systemic cycle's first phase, of material expansion, came to an end when the central power had accumulated more capital than established trade and production could absorb. This was followed by a second, financial phase of expansion in which capital overaccumulated at the center of the system promoted a new nucleus of growth. Ultimately the rising center came to finance the expenditures, often on war, that the old and now declining center could no longer cover out of its mere income.

It fits Arrighi's scheme that the US, having (along with the Chinese diaspora) once led international capital onto the Asian mainland, later became dependent on Chinese credit. For him, this announced the greatest switching crisis of all time, as China prepared to assume the hegemonic role reluctantly being relinquished by the US, and to inaugurate a new cycle of accumulation. Such a succession might ideally yield a new commonwealth of civilizations, in which capitalism as we know it would give way to what Arrighi somewhat hazily envisaged as a non-capitalist market economy recuperating old Chinese traditions of self-centered development. One condition of this happy scenario was that the United States abandon its armed imperialism and China remain committed to its "peaceful rise"; another, that the Chinese pioneer a green mode of growth distinct from "the Western, capital-intensive, energy-consuming path." Otherwise inter-imperial war, the ultimate means of competitive devaluation in *The Limits to Capital*, loomed once more.

In the recently published *Ecological Rift: Capitalism's War on the Earth*, John Bellamy Foster and his Marxist coauthors refer to the identification by a group of scientists, including the leading American climatologist James Hansen, of nine "planetary boundaries" that civilization transgresses at its peril. Already three—concentrations of carbon in the atmosphere, loss of nitrogen from the soil, and the overall extinction rate for nonhuman species—have been exceeded. These are impediments to endless capital accumulation that future crisis theories will have to reckon with. Harvey's intuition of the ultimate demise of capitalism has also taken on an ecological coloring. "Compound growth for ever"—historically, for capitalism, at about three percent a year—"is not possible," he declares in *The Enigma of Capital*, without much elaboration. The classical economists long ago foresaw that an economy defined by constant expansion would one day give way to what John Stuart Mill called the "stationary state." The idea has gained a new currency in Marxist writing of recent years, and in its contemporary version tends to locate the limits to growth in the depletion of natural resources or in the exhaustion of productivity gains as the share of manufacturing in the world economy shrinks and that of services expands. Of course, peak oil or soil exhaustion might easily coincide with faltering productivity. Harvey doesn't spell out why growth must have a stop, and the outlines of an ecologically stable and politically democratic future socialism remain as blurry in his later work as they do almost everywhere else. At the moment Marxism seems better prepared to interpret the world than to change it. But the first achievement is at least due wider recognition, which with the next crisis, or subsequent spasm of the present one, it may begin to receive.

February 2011

2

Fredric Jameson: The Cultural Logic of Neoliberalism

Fredric Jameson's preeminence, over the past generation, among critics writing in English would be hard to dispute. Part of the tribute has been exacted by his majestic style, one distinctive feature of which is the way that the convoy of long sentences freighted and balanced with subordinate clauses will dock here and there to unload a pithy slogan. "Always historicize!" is one of these, and Jameson has also insisted, under the banner of "One cannot *not* periodize," on the related necessity (as well as the semi-arbitrariness) of dividing history into periods. With that in mind, it's tempting to propose a period, coincident with Jameson's career as the main theorist of postmodernism, stretching from about 1983 (when Thatcher, having won a war, and Reagan, having survived a recession, consolidated their popularity) to 2008 (when the neoliberal program launched by Reagan and Thatcher was set back by the worst economic crisis since the Depression). During this period of neoliberal ascendancy—an era of deregulation, financialization, industrial decline, demoralization of the working class, the collapse of Communism and so on—it often seemed easier to spot the contradictions of Marxism than the more famous contradictions of capitalism, and no figure seemed to embody more than Fredric Jameson the peculiar condition of an economic theory that had turned out to flourish above all as a mode of cultural analysis, a mass movement that had become the province of an academic "elite," and an intellectual tradition that had arrived at some sort of culmination right at the point of apparent extinction.

Over the last quarter-century, Jameson has been at once the timeliest and most untimely of American critics and writers. Not only did he develop interests in film, science fiction, or the work of Walter Benjamin, say, earlier than most of his colleagues in the humanities, he was also a pioneer of that enlargement of literary criticism (Jameson received a PhD in French literature from Yale in 1959) into all-purpose *theory* which made the discussion of all these things in the same breath established academic practice. More than this, he succeeded better than anyone else at defining the term, "postmodernism," that sought to catch the historical specificity of the present age.

This was a matter, first, of cataloguing postmodernism's superficial textures: the erosion of the distinction between high and pop culture; the reign of stylistic pastiche and miscellany; the dominance of the visual image and corresponding eclipse of the written word; a new depthlessness— "surrealism without the unconscious"—in the dream-like jumble of images; and the strange alliance of a pervasive cultural nostalgia (as in the costume drama or historical novel) with a cultural amnesia serving to fragment "time into a series of perpetual presents." If all that now sounds familiar, this owes something to the durability of Jameson's account of postmodernism, first delivered as a lecture in 1982 and expanded two years later into an essay for *New Left Review*: a forty-page sketch that caught the features of the fidgety sitter more accurately than many longer studies before and since.

Jameson's description of the mood and texture of postmodern life had, in its almost tactile authority, few rivals outside the work of DeLillo, Pynchon and (more to his own taste) William Gibson. And, as in their novels, local observation in Jameson was complemented by an implacable awareness of what he called the "unrepresentable exterior" enclosing all the slick and streaming phenomena in view. In the novelists, however, allusion to the great ensphering system often took the form of paranoia. As a Marxist, Jameson was calmer and more forthright: he simply called the system "late capitalism," after the book by Ernest Mandel, the Belgian Trotskyist, which provided the base, as it were, to his own cultural superstructure. Mandel's *Late Capitalism* (1972) had offered a magnificently confident and pugnacious argument about the nature of postwar capitalism, but he regretted "not being able to propose a better term for this historical era than 'late capitalism.' " In Mandel's usage, "late" simply meant "recent," but the term naturally also suggests obsolescence. This implication of an utterly misplaced Marxist triumphalism probably had consequences for the reception of Jameson's theory (and Mandel's). Who could believe in 1991, when Jameson published *Postmodernism, Or, the Cultural Logic of Late Capitalism*, that capitalism was on its last legs?

In fact, Jameson didn't think it was either. His actual claim was more like the opposite: with the postwar elimination of precapitalist agriculture in the Third World and the last residue of feudal social relations in Europe, with the full commodification of culture (no more Rilke and Yeats and their noble patrons) and the infiltration of the old family-haunted unconscious by mass-disseminated images, humankind had only now embarked, for the first time, on a universally capitalist history. Late capitalism was the dawn, not the dusk, of a thoroughgoing capitalism. It constituted a "process in which the last surviving internal and external zones of precapitalism . . . are now ultimately penetrated and colonized in their turn." This thesis can only have been reinforced by the advent of China as the workshop of the world and the channeling of so much of intimate life by the internet. My shoes are sewn under the supervision of the CCP, and Gmail fills the margins of my private correspondence with ads.

And yet if Jameson owed to Marxism the special freshness of his insights, it was the same Marxism that made his work so untimely. He seems to have achieved notoriety as America's best-known Marxist in the years of the Soviet Union's death throes, when Marxism of any kind was held to be empirically disproved and indelibly tainted with mass murder. Moreover, his particular commitments went considerably beyond an axiomatic materialism in which economic conditions necessarily carve out whatever room for maneuver artists and writers enjoy; that much Marxism any liberal citizen might have accepted or even, under postmodernism, found impossible to deny. Far more suspect, during a period when utopia has been considered a euphemism for the Gulag, Jameson has also insisted time and again on the (usually unconscious) utopian element in all culture and politics, no matter how commercial the artifact or noxious the movement. The last words of his latest book, *Valences of the Dialectic,* maintain that "Utopia exists and that other systems, other spaces, are still possible."

Jameson's defense of the procedure he likes to call "totalization" has been in a similar vein. Totalization might be defined as the intellectual effort to recover the relationship between a given object—a novel, a film, a new building or a body of philosophical work—and the total historical situation underneath and around it. To contemporary ears, the term inevitably calls up associations with totalitarianism, and there is no denying that the method derives explicitly from the work of the Communist Lukács and the fellow-traveler Sartre, whom Jameson also failed to disown. Anathema to conservatives, the recourse to "totality" was no more endearing to a cultural left whose slogans included difference, heterotopia, nomadism, et cetera. This left seems to have faded from the American scene in recent years, but orthodox anti-Marxism looks unbudging. "Outside of a few university comparative literature departments," Anne Applebaum wrote recently in the *New York Review of Books*, "Soviet-style Marxism itself is not a living political idea anywhere in the West." (It's in "Soviet-style" that the real malice lies.) A few weeks later, a prominent science writer declared in a letter to the *New York Times* that "Marx's philosophy, put into practice, killed 30 million people through state-sponsored famines alone." The US remains a society in which Marxism can be advocated only a little more respectably than pederasty, and lately accusations of socialism erupt from the Republican Party more frequently than since McCarthy's heyday.

In *Late Marxism* (1990), his book on Adorno, Jameson wrote of *Dialectic of Enlightenment* that "the question about poetry after Auschwitz has been replaced with that of whether you could bear to read Adorno and Horkheimer next to the pool." With Jameson the question has been whether you could avoid reading him on a university campus, or continue reading him outside one. In Jonathan Franzen's *The Corrections* (2001), Chip Lambert, a former associate professor of literature in his thirties, decides to purge his library of Marxist cultural critics in order to raise some funds with which to indulge the yuppie tastes of his new girlfriend, Julia. Each of these books, Chip recalls, had once "called out" to him "with a promise of a radical critique of late capitalist society." And yet: "Theodor Adorno didn't have Julia's grapy smell of lecherous pliability, Fred Jameson didn't have Julia's artful tongue." Unburdened of his Marxist texts and their "reproachful spines," Chip proceeds to buy a fillet of "wild Norwegian salmon, line caught" for $78.40 at an upmarket grocery store Franzen calls the Nightmare of Consumption, a name to suggest that faced with the brazenness of yuppiedom (as by the 1990s it was no longer even called; it was just the way that almost anyone who could afford to be was) all satire or cultural criticism met defeat.

Jameson's *Postmodernism* had concluded with a call to "name the system." Ten years later, the system seemed to reply cheerfully to any ugly name you might call it. *Hi, I'm the Nightmare of Consumption. Nice to meet you!*

The Corrections, as well as being a far better novel than Jameson's strictures on an "exhausted realism" would suggest it could be, is a central instance of the literary populism that we can now recognize as one of the main trends of the American novel over the past decade or so. Franzen had no wish to be an obscure or difficult artist in the way that Adorno might have approved, and wasn't likely to mention Jameson without being able to trust that a good number of his readers would have some idea of who "Fred" was. Similarly, in Sam Lipsyte's new novel, *The Ask*, the forty-something narrator recalls that in college he learned about "late capitalism. And how to snort heroin." Interestingly, Lipsyte deals with the mediocre university where his narrator works in the same spirit of harassed literalism and defeated satire we can see in Franzen's Nightmare of Consumption: he calls the institution the Mediocre University. (Years ago, Jameson noticed a similar cynicism, operating from the other side, in the motto of *Forbes* magazine: "The Capitalist Tool.")

In both Franzen and Lipsyte the invocation of "late capitalism"—a term most people encountered in Jameson, not Mandel—is a mark of immaturity, an outworn college creed. The thing itself may grow old with us, but the term can't be used by middle-aged grown-ups participating in the real world (that is to say, the surface of the earth, minus college campuses). The same may go for "postmodernism," a word which by now provokes the weariness it once served in part to describe. What, then, of the writer whose own name is indissolubly linked to these terms? Jameson's latest book is about the dialectic, the unwieldy and now perhaps antique philosophical instrument invented by Hegel and handled back to front—a socialist tool—by Marx. A basic feature of dialectical thinking is the liability of subject and object to turn into each other, for the way a thing is looked at to become part of the look of the thing. Certainly that has been the case with Jameson himself and postmodernism: he became a landmark in the territory he had done so much to survey. The status of landmarks is ambiguous. Does a statue confirm the living influence of a man, or only that he belongs to the past?

It may not be too dialectical a characterization of the dialectician to say that Jameson's almost impossibly sophisticated variety of Marxist cultural criticism always wore the double aspect of a retreat and an advance. On the one hand, it appeared only to confirm the rout of the left that America's most famous Marxist was not a militant, a union boss or an economist, but a professor of literature and the author of learned and anfractuous prose whose essays contained untranslated blocks of French and bristling semiotic diagrams known as Greimas rectangles. What did anyone have to fear from Marxism if what had once been "a unity of theory and practice" was now chiefly a recondite species of book and movie criticism? Asylum in the literature department was surely just a prelude to an overdue extinction.

On the other hand, the Marxist tradition received in Jameson's work about as profound a vindication of its interpretative mission as could be imagined. It was one thing for him to insist—first in *The Political Unconscious* (1981)—that Marxism was the hermeneutic code that subsumed all others, that only in light of Marx's concept of the successive modes of production (hunting and gathering, early agriculture, feudalism and so on down to late capitalism) could the significance of any cultural or intellectual artifact be fully apprehended. But Jameson backed up the methodological boast in two ways.

First, with reserves of synthesizing energy that simply outstripped anyone else's, he was able to house within his own capacious and flexible scheme, like one of those skyscrapers that can bend in the wind, a remarkable number of newly important bodies of thought, including structuralist semiotics, *longue durée* history of the *Annales* variety, Frankfurt School *Kulturkritik* and the Marxian investigations of finance capital carried out by Giovanni Arrighi and David Harvey. One trait of postmodernism unmentioned by Jameson was the special difficulty critics and thinkers of recent generations have had in conveying their thoughts except through the medium of someone else's; intellectuals today tend to offer their commentary on the world by way of comments on another's commentary. Jameson has been unique, however, in his extremes of inclusion or ventriloquism. He seems to have detected some aspect of the truth in virtually any body of work he's discussed, and so to have recruited more, and more various, thinkers into the march of his own thoughts than any rival theorist. (Which means, among other things, that when he speculates about the fortunes of the great synthesizer Hegel in the years to come, it's equally the survival of his own way of thinking that's at issue.)

Second, starting in the early 1980s, Jameson produced what remains the most imposing account of the culture we all still inhabit. Postmodernism, he argued, did not spell the end of "metanarratives," as Lyotard had claimed. It was better understood as the recruitment of the entire world into the same big story, namely the development of global capitalism. (This marked a slight shift from his earlier claim that human history was already unified by the successive modes of production.) As for the self-referential quality of so much postmodern culture—language about language, images of images—this confirmed rather than contradicted the intimate relationship of culture to the heavy machinery of material production. The self-reflective idiom of post-modernism merely showed that specialization and the division of labor had seized the arts just as much as anything else; if culture increasingly talked about itself, this was because it talked increasingly *to* itself. In some ways, this was Max Weber's old insight, later elaborated as a logic of "differentiation" by the German systems theorist Niklas Luhmann, another writer often cited by Jameson: the apparent autonomy of various cultural activities or "value spheres" in reality reflected an increasingly unified and interconnected world. For Weber and Luhmann, modernity was the driver of this rationalization and differentiation. For Jameson, modernity, like postmodernity, was just another name for an evolving capitalism. (Marx himself had of course observed in *Capital* "how division of labor seizes upon, not only the economic, but every other sphere of society.") So did every weightless postmodern artifact in fact testify to the specific gravity of the fully capitalist planet it only appeared to float free of.

The wrinkle in this logic of differentiation was that, under postmodernism, there was also a lot of *de*-differentiation going on, as witness the merger of high and low culture, the mixing of styles within a given work, and even the tendency of "base" and "superstructure" to blur into one another. On this last point, Jameson has sometimes suggested that, given the patent fancifulness of the financialized economy—so much "fictitious capital" (as Marx called it) as disconnected from the "referent" of reality as the most delirious products of postmodernism—and the obvious subordination of contemporary culture to the bottom line, "the economic could be observed to have become cultural (just as the culture could be observed to become economic and commodified)." Theory as we've come to know it clearly offers another case of de-differentiation, in the breakdown of disciplinary boundaries between literary criticism, history, philosophy, anthropology and so on. With this in mind, Jameson has proposed a sort of homeopathic role for theory: intellectual de-differentiation countering the cultural/economic variety. At any rate, it shouldn't be too surprising to find so much differentiation and de-differentiation taking place side by side. You might draw an analogy with business practices, which shift between vertical integration, or doing everything within one company, and subcontracting, in which tasks are farmed out.

All together, the sophistication of Jameson's work and the breadth of his references had a dual effect. He wrote stirringly of the vocation of "dialectical philosophy and Marxism" to "break out of the specialized compartments of the (bourgeois) disciplines and to make connections among the seemingly disparate phenomena of social life generally," and clearly his own work belonged to and even crowned this Western Marxist lineage. Behind his project lay the understanding that social life is "a seamless web, a single inconceivable and transindividual process, in which there is no need to invent ways of linking language events and social upheavals or economic contradictions because on that level they were never separate from one another." And yet for Jameson to shepherd so many other theories and so much of contemporary culture into the big tent of his own theory could only be the task of a rare intelligence singularly devoted to the project. Such de-differentiation, in other words, was the fruit of a profound differentiation; all this totalizing had to be purchased at the expense of what Marx called that "all engrossing system of specializing and sorting men, that development in a man of one single faculty at the expense of all others." Intellectually, Jameson was central. Socially, such a figure can hardly have been more marginal and "elite," something that has become truer with each passing decade.

Jameson has been a professor mostly at Duke, toniest of southern colleges. And you could say that American higher education itself suffered a dialectical reversal somewhere around 1980—to date, the high-water mark of class mobility in the US—as the universities went from being among the main vehicles of egalitarianism to being the primary means of reproducing class privilege. Everyone talks, with good reason, about the runaway costs of healthcare in America, but if healthcare inflation since 1980 has exceeded 400 percent, the price of a university education has risen, on a recent calculation, by an incredible 827 percent. Jameson's Marxism might have been rare enough in any circumstances, but forces beyond his control also had the effect of making it seem outrageously *expensive*. Jameson recognized the problem: "What is socially offensive about 'theoretical' texts like my own," he said in an interview, is "not their inherent difficulty, but rather the signals of higher education, that is, of class privilege, which they emit." But of course he couldn't solve it.

The dialectic, Jameson explains in the new book, has among its main tasks the recovery of the common situation binding together thoughts or realities that seem on the face of it to have nothing in common—just the operation that he has often defended under the name of "totalization." He illustrates the idea with a famous example from Hegel: "Thus, the Slave is not the opposite of the Master, but rather, along with him, an equally integral component of the larger system called slavery or domination." This is a simple instance, since no special ingenuity is required to see that you can't have slaves without masters or vice versa. It's perhaps not much harder to grasp the idea of Fredric Jameson and someone like Sarah Palin as two faces of the same coin, figures truly as absurd as their opponents make them out to be, but only because the system itself is utterly cracked. So intellectual debility becomes a badge of populism, and socialist learning a hobby of rich people's children.

Common, probably, to most favorable and unfavorable impressions of Jameson has been the image of him as an author of forbidding treatises, massive salt licks of theory. Undeniably, many of the books *are* thick, including *Valences of the Dialectic*, a doorstop of some 600 pages. As with Jameson's previous book, *The Ideologies of Theory* (2009), the title alone brandishes two words that, in the US at least, can hardly be used in polite—which is to say, anti-intellectual—company. Reading *Valences of the Dialectic* on the subway I felt more sheepish than I had since bringing Gregor von Rezzori's (ironically titled!) *Memoirs of an Anti-Semite* on board.

The impression of Jameson's erudition was never wrong, nor the sense that he could be a difficult writer. But it was a mistake to perceive him as the architect of colossal tomes. The longest of his books are in reality sheaves of essays; his original pages on postmodernism, though they would later be inserted into a great silver-blue volume ten times as long, show a pamphleteer's provisional and exuberant spirit. But the postmodern age hasn't been a pamphleteering one, and the left-wing journals in which Jameson's articles have mostly appeared address an even narrower audience than the cultural studies section of an independent bookstore. Still, it's more accurate to see Jameson as a writer of long essays than of long books. And the essays themselves regain their polemical sharpness and definition when considered in isolation and not as the chapters of so many books.

Two new essays, freshly composed for the occasion, bookend *Valences of the Dialectic*; in between are mainly reprints of pieces many of which don't concern or exhibit dialectical thinking much more (or any less) than the rest of Jameson's work in the years since he published "Toward a Dialectical Criticism" in *Marxism and Form* in 1971. Of the bookends, the first offers a provisional introduction to the dialectic. That neither it nor the volume as a whole is meant to stand as definitive is made clear by a slightly comic footnote in which Jameson, regretting the lack of "the central chapter on Marx and his dialectic which was to have been expected," promises two future volumes, on Hegel and Marx respectively, to "complete the project." Meanwhile (a favorite Jamesonian transition, as if everything was present in his mind all at once, and it was only the unfortunately sequential nature of language that forced him to spell out sentence by sentence and essay by essay an apprehension of the contemporary world that was simultaneous and total), it may further correct the idea of him as a tome-monger to point out that such a mood of provisionality or hesitation runs throughout his work. For all the consistency of his commitments, he has not produced worked-out arguments and scholarly findings so much as a tissue of hints, hypotheses, recommendations and impressions. It would be easy to find many sentences in Jameson starting like this one: "Now we may begin to hazard the guess that something like the dialectic will always begin to appear when thinking approaches the dilemma of incom-mensurability . . ." Such accumulated qualifications—and yet "always." The effect here may approach self-parody, but that is a hazard no truly distinctive stylist avoids. Not often in American writing since Henry James can there have been a mind displaying at once such tentativeness and force.

Jameson's preference for a conditional over a declarative mood is a token of the necessarily speculative quality of what he does. It's far easier to be sure that culture is indeed mediat-ing the economy than to establish in any given case how such mediation works. In *Valences of the Dialectic*, one of the most striking suggestions made in the introductory essay is that Hegel, who articulated his omnivorous philosophical logic at a time when industrial capitalism was hardly more than a local English affair, may have been seized by an intimation of the ultimately global logic of capitalism: capitalism too is forever enlarging itself, and bringing under one rule the most disparate people and places. So does creative destruction on the economic plane resemble the dialectic's refusal to freeze or reify its concepts and stand pat. Dialectical thought, then, would be at once the mirror of capitalism and (in Marxist hands) its rival: the totalizing imperative that is the dialectic confronting the totality that is capitalism. From this it follows that the dialectic, despite the musty air of the word, may be set to come into its own only today, with the universal instal-lation of capitalism. The thought may be less outrageous than it appears. After all, it was an explicitly Hegelian formu-lation—the end of history—that captured for the public imagination the meaning of the collapse of Communism in

Europe. Jameson's reiterated Marxist reply is simply that the disappearance of the Second World and the elimination of pre-capitalist arrangements in the Third marks in fact the *beginning* of a universal history: "History, which was once multiple, is now more than ever unified into a single History." In characteristic Jamesonian fashion, the stray hints and speculations gather themselves, towards the end of *Valences*, into a stark and audacious proposition: "The worldwide triumph of capitalism . . . secures the priority of Marxism as the ultimate horizon of thought in our time." How's that for dialectical?

The particular "dilemma of incommensurability" preoccupying Jameson in the long concluding essay of *Valences* concerns the disjunction of biological or existential time (one's threescore and ten) with the differently experienced time of History. By History, Jameson means the succession of the happy or unhappy destinies of whole peoples and classes within the "single vast unfinished plot"—as he put it almost thirty years ago in *The Political Unconscious*—of humankind's existence. Of course individual experience and collective fate consist in the same living substance, but the sensation of their identity, "a recognition of our ultimate Being as History," is a rare and fleeting glimpse into the demographic sublime—all those suffering persons dead, living and still unborn—too dizzying and appalling to be sustained.

Jameson has argued for years that the intersection of existential and historical time has become particularly rare in postmodern times. In spite of the obvious historical novelty of our present way of life, the past tends to fall rapidly away into oblivion or else to be taken up by media representations that serve as "the very agents and mechanisms for our historical amnesia." The result, as he put it in his great essay "The Antinomies of Postmodernity" in *The Seeds of Time* (1994), was that "for us time consists in an eternal present and, much further away, an inevitable catastrophe, these two moments showing up distinctly on the registering apparatus without overlapping or transitional states."

No one, it seems to me, has better conveyed the oddly becalmed quality of recent decades, the sense of a "locked social geology so massive that no visions of modification seem possible (at least to those ephemeral biological subjects that we are)." It was in the light of the feeling of a windless postmodern stasis that Jameson wanted to stick up for utopianism, especially in *Archaeologies of the Future* (2005), his appreciation of utopia as a subgenre of science fiction and an immortal human desire: "The very political weakness of utopia in previous generations—namely that it furnished nothing like an account of agency, nor did it have a coherent historical and practical-political picture of transition—now becomes a strength in a situation in which neither of these problems seems currently to offer candidates for a solution." The dialectic, Adorno said, would renounce itself if it renounced the "idea of potentiality," and it was just this dimension that Jameson meant to preserve amid the deadly consensus as to the unsurpassable virtues of liberal capitalism.

In "The Valences of History," the concluding essay of the new book, Jameson argues that when the fitful apprehension of history does enter the lives of individuals it is often through the feeling of belonging to a particular generation: "The experience of generationality is . . . a specific collective experience of the present: it marks the enlargement of my existential present into a collective and historical one." A generation, he adds, is not forged by passive endurance of events, but by hazarding a collective project. That this too is uncommon enough can be deduced from Jameson's example of the process: "Avant-gardes are so to speak the voluntaristic affirmation of the generation by sheer willpower, the allegories of a generational mission that may never come into being." So the small sect crystallizes the would-be universal—an ironic and possibly dialectical contradiction, and a fitting suggestion for a Marxist professor to make amid a near unchallenged global capitalism.

The theme of generations recurs from time to time in Jameson, whose work in any case proceeds less by straightforward argumentation than by a kaleidoscopic rotation across a consistent set of problems. In "Periodizing the 60s" (1984), he noted that "the classification by generations has become as meaningful for us as it was for the Russians of the late nineteenth century, who sorted character types out with reference to specific decades," and in that essay and elsewhere this rigorously non-confessional writer has hinted at the decisive importance of the 1960s in his own formation. Jameson's fellow Marxist critics Perry Anderson and Terry Eagleton (with some cosmic design evidently at work in the similarity of all three names) have already testified to his eminence in such a way as to give some sense of his importance to their own generation. It is a generation in which a younger person notices, though not especially among the Marxists, a widespread and not infrequently pathetic tendency toward serial intellectual and cultural faddism, which makes it the more impressive and even inspiring—to Jameson's peers as well, it may be—that he has stayed true to the utopian stirrings of the 1960s while remaining open to so much of what's come since.

Jameson once likened the goofy eclecticism of certain postmodern architecture to the recipes inspired by "late-night reefer munchies," and it may be an observation to bridge the gap between his generation, steeped in the 1960s, and my own to say that reading Jameson himself has always reminded me a bit of being on drugs. The less exceptional essays were like being stoned: it all seemed very profound at the time, but the next day you could barely remember a thing. Indeed there's no other author I've frequented or admired to the same degree so many of whose pages produced absolutely no impression on me. And yet the best of Jameson's work has felt mind-blowing in the way of LSD or mushrooms: here before you is the world you'd always known you were living in, but apprehended as if for the first time in the freshness of its beauty and horror. One of the trippier as well as more affecting passages in *Valences of the Dialectic* is a sort of aria on the condition of living, through global capitalism, in a totally man-made world, one in which even the weather patterns and the geological age (the Anthropocene, it was recently declared) are human productions:

We have indeed secreted a human age out of ourselves as spiders secrete their webs: an immense, all-encompassing ceiling . . . which shuts down visibility on all sides even as it absorbs all the formerly natural elements in its habitat, transmuting them into its own man-made substance. Yet within this horizon of immanence we wander as alien as tribal people, or as visitors from outer space, admiring its unimaginably complex and fragile filigree and recoiling from its bottomless potholes, lounging against a rainwall of exotic and artificial plants or else agonizing among poisonous colors and lethal stems we were not taught to avoid. The world of the human age is an aesthetic pretext for grinding terror or pathological ecstasy, and in its cosmos, all of it drawn from the very fibers of our own being and at one with every post-natural cell more alien to us than nature itself, we continue murmuring Kant's old questions—What can I know? What should I do? What may I hope?—under a starry heaven no more responsive than a mirror or a spaceship, not understanding that they require the adjunct of an ugly and bureaucratic representational qualification: what can I know *in this system*? What should I do in this world *completely invented by me*? What can I hope for alone in an *altogether human age*?

In such a passage it's possible to see a few things. One is as much evidence as a few lines could offer for placing Jameson among the important American writers of the age *tout court*. Another is his special way of being one of those (to vary what Henry James said) by whom nothing is abandoned: the apprehension of the alienness of the world is the signature experience in Sartre's *Nausea*, whose author was the subject of Jameson's PhD thesis and first book; the "human age" alludes to the trilogy of novels by Wyndham Lewis, subject of another book-length study by Jameson; and the situation described here, of humanity confronting its own handiwork as something alien and exterior, is very much that of Marx's alienated labor, in which the worker is dominated by the product of his own hands, his estranged "species-being" ranged against him in the form of someone else's capital. But the reader's impression of tremendous intellectual power is accompanied by one of political paralysis. Who is this collective human "I," in a world "completely invented by me"? Nobody at all. Again, the analogy with drugs: perceptual journeys across the universe, confined to the couch.

My impression is that it's this combination of hypertrophied theory and atrophied "praxis" in Jameson that causes his name to provoke as many smirks as sighs of admiration. But from the point of view that he has so imposingly established and defended it would be a bit moralizing, individualistic and certainly undialectical to judge whether it was good or bad that Marxism has taken the form it does in his work. The most intelligible Marxist account of individual greatness in a writer or artist is that it belongs to the figure who opens himself unreservedly to the sociohistorical forces in play. "The intervening individual subject," Adorno wrote in *Aesthetic Theory* (1970), "is scarcely more than a limiting value, something minimal required by the artwork for its crystallization." Jameson's tremendous cultural and intellectual receptivity would alone seem enough to certify his achievement. In what rival body of work is there more of the contemporary world to see? And how can he be taxed with failing to formulate a political program not on offer anywhere else? It is already a substantial feat to have preserved and extended the legacy of Marxism for a generation of intellectuals in which it might otherwise have nearly expired.

What now? The near consensus that obtained for a quarter-century on politics and economics, leaving culture as the real terrain of battle, has faltered over the past few years. What does this do to Jameson's work? One threat to his legacy is that it's hard to imagine any of his inheritors excelling him in sophistication. Perry Anderson has hailed Jameson as the culmination of Western Marxism. In literary history, culminations—of, say, the psychological novel in Proust, or Romantic poetry in Yeats, or a certain modernism in Beckett—often look like dead ends. And why would going further be necessary? Jameson himself has suggested that in light of the obvious instability and injustice of global capitalism, a perfectly vulgar Marxism might these days do just as well.

The relative neglect of strictly economic questions in Jameson (and in Western Marxism generally) also now looks like a liability. After all, the recent implosion of the markets, and efficient-market theory with them, hasn't induced a stampede in the direction of Marxism. The crisis revived interest in Keynes and Minsky, but it will apparently take until the next convulsion, or longer, for the same to happen to Marx the economist, and the writers from Hilferding to Harvey who worked out Marxian theories of finance.

Of course it would contradict Jameson's account of how culture works if his own writing didn't reproduce some of the blind spots he detects in the world at large, where material production seems somehow to be hidden from view and where social transformation has looked like a dead letter. Still, the weak point in his strongly Marxist account of recent culture has been his relatively thin description of the economy, the mode of production. It is too easy to read much of his work and conclude that a given film or novel could indeed be read as a blind allegory of "late capitalism," without late capitalism meaning anything much more distinct than "the economy" or "the system." In such cases it has been far easier to accept his Marxism in an axiomatic sense—a product of late capitalism will necessarily be *about* late capitalism too— than to see how the axiom could be embodied in persuasive local analyses of this or that cultural artifact or tendency.

And yet it isn't as if Jameson can't do that too. Some of his strongest essays, for instance "The Brick and the Balloon" (1998) or "The End of Temporality" (2003)—about, respectively, postmodern architecture and the waning contemporary sense of past and future—analyze these phenomena the more convincingly and illuminatingly for doing so in the context of the bodiless and instantaneous transactions of finance capital. It would only have enriched Jameson's work if he had directed his attention to the cultural fallout of other novel features of the latest stage of capitalism: Mandel mentioned not only computerization and the rise of the service industries, themes Jameson has occasionally taken up, but also accelerated turnover time for fixed capital (i.e. a shorter period in which to recoup one's investment), and the replacement of the gold standard by floating currencies. It's not hard to imagine these transformations of the base percolating up through the superstructure. The mass introduction of women into the paid workforce, the expansion of advertizable space, the displacement of cash by credit cards and digital transactions: these are a few of the other economic changes in recent decades that come to mind as having suffused the superstructure too. Perhaps the outstanding virtue of David Harvey's *Condition of Postmodernity* (1989) was his correlation of sped-up cultural change with a general "space-time compression" operating in contemporary capitalism across such disparate features as a casualized labor market, expanded international trade, shorter-term investment and so on—though it should be added that Harvey's work along these lines followed Jameson's and might not have been possible without it.

Jameson has often written of a given stage of capitalism setting the "conditions of possibility" within which a writer or artist has to work. It might equally be said of his own work as a critic that it established the conditions of possibility for a Marxist cultural criticism at least as often as it offered an example of such a thing. Here, then, is another of Jameson's contradictions: sighing with cultural belatedness, his essays have also seemed like preludes, prolegomena, to work yet to be done. Whether this work will use the word "postmodernism" doesn't seem very important. In fact it's probably worth remembering Jameson's "therapeutic" recommendation, at the end of *A Singular Modernity* (2002), that capitalism might be substituted "for modernity in all the contexts in which the latter appears," and extending the suggestion to postmodernity too. That would place us squarely in the midst of a capitalist or (to periodize a bit more) neoliberal culture, waiting to see what comes next. It would also place us in Jameson's debt.

April 2010

3

Robert Brenner: Full Employment and the Long Downturn

The inherent right to work is one of the elemental privileges of a free people.

—FDR, radio address, 1937

Of all classic capitalist problems—income inequality, imperialism, the class character of the state, and so on—mass unemployment has probably been the one to trouble living Americans least. From the establishment of FDR's war economy through the end of the so-called Golden Age of capitalism in the early 1970s, the US matched other major economies in functioning at close to full employment (at least as the term is defined by economic orthodoxy, on which more later). In the troughs of recessions, the unemployment rate might touch 7 percent, but otherwise it wavered between about 3 and 5.5. And even with the onset in 1973 of what Robert Brenner, in the commanding economic history of the period, called the "long downturn"—a decline across the system in rates of growth and profit, persisting to this day—the US touted a distinctly better record of job creation than its main European rivals. The average unemployment rate for the '70s came to slightly above 6 percent; for the '80s, above 7; and for the '90s, just below 6—a marked deterioration since the end of the Golden Age, but not bad by international standards. The years from 1997 to 2006 saw an average stateside rate below 5 percent, achieved though this was with the decisive aid of serial financial bubbles.

Europe has never dispersed the cloud of structural unemployment that settled over the '70s. France, Germany, Italy, and Spain registered unemployment rates around 10 percent as late into the last expansion as 2004, and last year's recession has erased most gains since then across the Continent. The situation remains far worse in poor countries, whose vast cities have never gathered into formal paid employment the populations displaced from the land by the postwar commercialization of agriculture. As a result, some two-fifths of economically active humanity now ekes out its subsistence in an "informal sector"—essentially a euphemism for unemployment—often marked by salvage, racketeering, and violence.

Of course the relatively attractive American figures ignored a massive prison population, which—starting its steep ascent, suspiciously enough, in the mid-1970s—now exceeds 2.4 million, mostly men of working age. Reckoning these disproportionately black and Latino inmates, short on marketable skills—in other words, the very people with the worst job prospects—into the official unemployment rate would raise it by about a percent and a half. And other cases of concealed unemployment abound among cohabiting couples and young people living at home; for obvious reasons, they can give up searching for a job more easily than adults on their own. Had these and other "discouraged workers" been counted as unemployed, and had the official numbers included part-timers wishing to be full-time, 1997's proud 4.7 percent rate would have been more like 7 or, counting prisoners, 9: a thought to salt any moist nostalgia for the good old days of Clintonomics.

It's also worth keeping in mind the actual contours of an American job. American employees spend more hours at work than their European or Japanese counterparts; their two weeks of vacation are the least in the rich world; many jobs don't include health benefits; those that do, deprive workers of health care should they become unemployed (a powerful instrument of labor discipline); maternity leave, when women feel they can take it at all without imperiling job security, is minimal by first-world standards; and the crumbling legal standard of the eight-hour day doesn't actually set much limit on exploitation: nothing stipulates that you can't work two such jobs. The minimum wage, capable as late as 1980 of supporting a full-time worker at the poverty line, has now fallen 40 percent beneath that level. Among badly paid and often undocumented workers in trades like construction and meat-packing, industrial accidents run into the hundreds of thousands each year, the more so since the Bush administration cut the budget of the Occupational Safety and Hazard Administration each year of its tenure. At the opposite end of the pay spectrum, the advent of smart phones and laptops has put many white-collar workers perpetually on call in a way formerly reserved for doctors and firemen. And it goes almost without saying that the celebrated "flexibility" of the US labor market is an honorific for casual dismissal. Yet in spite of these ungenerous conditions—or, if you listen to the business press, precisely *because* the American model refuses to coddle workers—the US had for more than thirty years distinguished itself as the large economy, outside of Japan, in which it was easiest to find a job: an ambiguous achievement but a real one.

The American approximation to "full employment" has now collapsed. In the aftermath of the recession, which may well double-dip, unemployment hovers around 10 percent. The U-6 or "true unemployment rate," which includes some discouraged workers as well as unwilling part-timers, stands near 17 percent. A smaller proportion of workers between the ages of sixteen and twenty-four is employed than at any time since the Depression. The probability of an unemployed person finding work over the next month, ordinarily about one in three during recessions, has sunk to one in five.* Recent polls find alarmingly but not unexpectedly high rates of stress, anger, and depression among laid-off workers; the wages of unemployment are material deprivation and psychic pain.

According to the Federal Reserve, unemployment will remain above 7 percent through the end of 2012: a cold new floor perhaps, where the Golden Age had placed a ceiling.

---

* Doug Henwood's calculation, applying a statistical measure developed by the economist Robert Shimer.

The likelihood is that the end of a period of severe cyclical unemployment will disclose a new landscape of permanent unemployment, with jobs in manufacturing, construction, and finance having been eliminated without equivalent new openings in other industries. Trends toward outsourcing and automation augur even worse conditions: a quarter of American jobs are said to be exportable, and another sizable fraction must be expendable in favor of technology. In principle, none of this requires increased long-term unemployment. If a given task will now be performed in another country or by a machine, it doesn't follow that there is no further economic use for the person thus replaced. But the system-wide tendency, for almost four decades now, has been to add jobs more slowly than population, and there is no reason to think that, absent a political movement for true full employment, the US will avoid the fate of the rest of the capitalist world: a place—now a planet—where a proportionally shrinking body of laborers is ever more heavily exploited to ensure a rate of profit that nevertheless continually declines.

Our political demand should be for the opposite arrangement: a larger mass of labor more lightly exploited. The ultimate goal is a job for everyone who wants and can perform one. On the face of it, this is not a controversial program. Full employment is one of those political ideals, like democracy, that almost everyone claims to admire; no important strain of economics fails to promote it in name. So you might suppose that the near achievement of full employment during the Golden Age or "long boom" (Brenner) from the late '40s through the early '70s would be counted among the triumphs of the period. In fact, the opposite is true. For left and mainstream economists alike, full employment has most often been seen as the snake in the garden of postwar prosperity, and the ultimate cause of its demise. The theory is simple enough: full employment raised wages to a level at which they cut too deeply into profits. Businesses could only react by raising consumer prices, leading workers to seek still higher wages. Inflation spiraled upward; profitability still faltered; and economies slid toward stagnation. The only way, then, to preserve "full employment" was to redefine it as an ideal rate of *unemployment*, just enough so that inflation would not increase. The scope of any left agenda this side of socialism depends on whether we retain this definition of full employment, and what answer we give to the related question of how the Golden Age turned leaden.

The historical controversy can come first. What was the Golden Age that full employment could have put an end to it? The first decades after World War II saw not only high rates of overall growth and profitability, hence their auriferous name, but also tremendous productivity growth (measured in output per hour) and a rapid expansion of labor markets across the wealthier countries. Accelerated automation, along with new efficiencies in transportation and electricity generation, allowed more commodities to be produced in the same amount of time. This made commodities cheaper, which in turn meant that real wages could rise while what Marxism call the rate of exploitation (the ratio of profits to wages) also went up. Meanwhile the flood of women and young people onto the job market relieved any tendency to labor scarcity; the number of American women doing paid labor grew by 71 percent between 1950 and 1970, and the number of teenagers by nearly as much. Since most of these new workers were not (or weren't imagined to be) heads of households, they were unable to demand a living wage and could be hired at low cost.

By the early '70s, on standard accounts, dwindling rates of technological innovation were converging in the US and elsewhere with the saturation of the labor market. Neither increased productivity nor a flow of new workers could be relied on to keep wages from growing more slowly—or at least no more quickly—than profits; both streams were drying up. Despite its Marxist vocabulary, the argument of Ernest Mandel in *Late Capitalism* (1972) coincides with prevailing views ever since:

> As soon as expansion led to the dismantling and disappearance of the industrial reserve army [Marx's term for the unemployed] . . . the golden years of late capitalism were internationally over. There was no longer any chance of an automatic increase in the rate of profit or its maintenance at a high level. *The struggle over the rate of surplus-value* [the ratio of profits to wages: in practice, synonymous with the rate of exploitation] *now flared up anew.* Moreover, in this struggle it was precisely the high level of employment which contributed to a significant increase in the strength of wage-earners . . . Late capitalism cannot

avoid a period of relatively decelerated economic expansion if it fails to break the resistance of wage-earners and so to achieve a new radical increase in the rate of surplus-value. (Mandel's emphasis)

The argument attributes the diminished economic vitality of the '70s to a profit squeeze induced by excessively high wages attendant on full employment. "The strength of wage-earners" curtailed profits, which in turn reduced business investment. A certain debate flourishes as to whether lower business investment led, then, to further declines in productivity, as R&D budgets were cut and new technologies could not be developed and applied, or whether, instead, the technological potential of the Golden Age was simply being exhausted: past a certain point, and regardless of investment, assembly lines can't become much more automated or rationalized. Either way, the proposition that the wage bill of a fully employed population made it impossible to sustain prior rates of growth and profitability has been common to neoliberals in Chicago, Keynesians in Berkeley, and Marxists in greater London.

Robert Brenner, in *The Economics of Global Turbulence* (2006), calls this the Full Employment Profit Squeeze thesis. The thesis has proved remarkably durable in the face of the stubborn persistence, since the '70s, of weak economic performance among the rich countries—even with the return of mass unemployment, the worldwide enfeeblement of the labor movement, and the stagnation or outright decline of real wages. How can the effect of slower growth have so outlived its notorious cause? According to the thesis, post–Golden Age workers still enjoy too much power at the levels of shop floor, industry, and government. To risk full employment in these circumstances would only unleash another wage explosion, with labor costs again outrunning productivity. The restoration of the system's dynamism can only come about through labor's final defeat or surrender—one that, in spite of all of labor's lost battles over the last thirty years, still has yet to occur. Further reductions in real wages, further erosion of unemployment benefits, and increased economic insecurity constitute the recipe for profitability. If the US has logged higher growth and fuller employment over the last twenty years than other advanced economies, this owes to its greater, if still incomplete, acceptance of these home truths.

Inevitably this view claims many adherents among overlapping schools of libertarians, Austrophiles, and marginalists, for whom all interference in the market, including a legal minimum wage, is a crime against prosperity. Thus the return of mass joblessness to America has prompted op-ed pages on the right and several notable economists to bay for the reduction of the minimum wage as a means to full employment. But the argument that labor has still failed to accommodate itself to the requirements of capital accumulation knows its left versions as well. In a 1996 overview of "Social Democracy and Full Employment" in *New Left Review*, the late British economist Andrew Glyn, a pioneer of the profit squeeze thesis, concluded that "the slowdown after 1973, above all of investment, was the response to rising inflation and profit squeeze . . . In such a context of weak private demand and slow productivity growth, maintaining full employment required severe restraint on workers' pay and consumption to keep exports competitive, investment profitable and the budget under control." In this analysis, shared in essence by Barry Eichengreen's impressive study of *The European Economy Since 1945* (2006), the labor movement in Europe failed to impose on itself the necessary wage restraint. Note, however, the question-begging role of "weak private demand" in Glyn's sketch of post-1970s malaise. Surely if private consumer demand is too weak this cannot be because wages run too high? And—another crucial question—is the competitive pricing of exports really a sine qua non of social democracy?

Setting aside these doubts for the moment, it is at least obvious that the Full Employment Profit Squeeze thesis no longer holds much political allure for the left. If Marxists during the '70s could relish the imminent apocalyptic showdown between labor and capital it promised, that day is gone. Many features of Mandel's *Late Capitalism* hold up remarkably well against the background of later developments, but the herald of impending revolution with which he ended his book, summoning "the mass revolutionary movement of the international working class that is now approaching," could hardly have a more antique ring to it. If a contest over wages and profits has to be resolved today by either the reduction of the former through a lowered standard of living, or the final elimination of the latter through the transcendence of capitalism, one possibility sounds like what you might read about in tomorrow's paper and the other like a pipedream.

Today, the profit-squeeze thesis has become a very bitter pill, to be swallowed without any chaser of revolutionary hopes. It would mean acceding to calls for still lower wages, and accepting still more income inequality and social insecurity as the ransom for future growth. You would want to be sure the prescription of this harsh medicine was correct. You might therefore seek a second opinion.

Much of the originality of Brenner's *Economics of Global Turbulence* lies in its frontal attack on the idea of wage-induced profit squeeze. For Brenner, not excessive wages but the maturation of international competition in manufacturing produced the long downturn. As Germany and Japan in the '60s and '70s, the "newly industrializing countries" of East Asia in the '80s and '90s, and finally the Chinese colossus of today intruded upon the markets of prior industrial powers, increased competition exerted relentless downward pressure on profits, resulting in diminished business investment, reduced payrolls, and—with lower R&D expenditure—declining productivity gains from technological advance. The textbook result of this industrial tournament would have been the elimination of less competitive firms. But the picture drawn by *The Economics of Global Turbulence* is one of "excessive entry and insufficient exit" in manufacturing. Brenner argues that with so much money sunk in expensive plants and campuses, it was often more rational for firms to accept a below-average rate of return than to close up shop and suffer the wholesale devaluation of their fixed capital. So relatively unprofitable firms hung on for dear life, bringing down the average health of the system. In such a climate of weak industrial profitability, available capital increasingly chose a fleet-footed speculative career over more rooted investment in manufacturing. Hence the financialization of the world economy, delivering more volatility than growth.

To this original argument about the causes of the long downturn corresponds an equally heterodox vision of its possible overcoming. If the restoration-through-crisis proposed by the profit squeeze thesis entails further concessions from labor, Brenner has in mind a different purgative: the severe winnowing of high-cost, low-profit manufacturers across the globe. Liberated thus from mutually destructive competition, surviving firms and freed-up capital could regain the high profit rates that would enable them to lead an international expansion. Brenner doesn't suggest that such a "shakeout" would spare workers (or capital) enormous pain, but for him it offers the sole prospect for revival within the terms of the current system. Those terms include unrestricted capital mobility and, as for Glyn, export-oriented growth among later-developing economies.

The opposition between the standard profit-squeeze argument and Brenner's position is stark. The former presents a vision of excessive competition of workers with capital; the latter, of excessive competition among what Marx called "the many capitals." From a political standpoint, Brenner's anatomy of the long downturn at first looks more inviting. Who on the left wouldn't prefer a rash of corporate bankruptcies to the kneecapping of living standards? But *The Economics of Global Turbulence* is formidable not only for its unrivaled command of the relevant data and its comparative perspective—treating the shifting fortunes of the American, German, and Japanese economies as no other work has done—but also for its saturnine mood. For Brenner, the problems of contemporary capitalism brook no adjustment. The temporary triumph of some important firms and the destruction of others might set the stage for higher rates of growth, but this growth would take off, after a vast "slaughter of capital values" (as Marx once put it), from a lower plane of overall prosperity. The abandonment of American factories could only accelerate, and the unemployment rate with it. Even then, following a bout of creative destruction the likes of which the world has never seen, the result would presumably be, though Brenner doesn't say so, the eventual reemergence of overcompetition and incipient global stagnation.

The strength of this vision lies in its treatment of the great supposed virtue of contemporary capitalism—unfettered international competition—as its deadly vice. Out of a historian's tact or a socialist's despair, Brenner never implies the possibility of any tolerable reform of the system or lets slip a prayer for revolution. The main body of *The Economics of Global Turbulence* appeared as a special edition of *New Left Review* in 1998, in the heyday of Clinton and Blair's "third way," with the socialist parties of Europe having converted to neoliberalism and Communist China embarked on its great program of underpricing foreign labor, and before the turn to the left across South America. Here, one is tempted to say, is the Marxism, without comfort for labor or laurels for capital, that the '90s deserved.

And yet: Doesn't Brenner's position acquire a more hopeful cast if you consider its unstated implications regarding consumer demand? The problem he identifies of industrial overcapacity and overproduction—of too much plant producing too many goods—is manifestly one of excess supply. And excess supply can presumably be addressed in one of two ways: by reducing supply to the level of demand (through the envisioned shakeout of uncompetitive firms), or by raising demand to the level of supply. Excess capacity would disappear with the circumstance of adequate overall demand. In this sense, the fatally overpaid workers of the past forty years, as they have been conceived of across the political spectrum, might be reconceived as fatally *underpaid*, not just from their own point of view but from the standpoint of systemic requirements for sustained growth.

To draw this consequence from Brenner's argument is to turn the received idea of the Golden Age on its head. After all, even in the legendary days of "full employment" joblessness in the US was often three or four times higher than in Sweden, and Johnson's War on Poverty hardly named a phantom enemy; it was never the case that all who wanted a job could get one, or that fear of hardship had ceased to exert its discipline. Might it be that the era's fatal flaw lay not in excess compensation for workers and over-full employment, but in insufficient wage growth and not-full-enough employment?

Resurrecting the old Marxist measure of the rate of exploitation—which no one seems to try to calculate anymore—would probably support the idea that inadequate rather than excessive wages and employment sapped the Golden Age. Mandel's work showed that throughout the '50s and '60s the rate of exploitation (again, the proportion of profits to wages) ran at a high level. This very imbalance permitted the thirty years' truce between capital and labor; though real wages were rising fast, profits rose even faster. And yet, as readers of Marx know, a high rate of exploitation poses a potential problem of *realization*. If would-be purchasers are held back by low wages, then the total mass of commodities cannot be unloaded at the desired price. Capital fails to realize its customary profit, and accumulation toward stagnation.

What, after all, can be done with increasing profits? A portion flows into the consumption fund of wealthy households, and it is conceivable that the rich could spend enough to maintain a sufficient level of consumer demand. (The US approached just such a strategy over the last dozen years, with help from the delirious increase of asset prices.) But as Keynes pointed out, the proportion of income going to consumption tends to decline as incomes rise across social classes. For this reason it would be reckless, never mind grotesque, to rely on rich people's appetite for luxuries to make up for a general shortfall in demand. In practice, a substantial portion of the income of wealthy households tends to be saved, which is to say invested and restored to its status as capital.

By definition, capital seeks to realize at least the average rate of profit. How should it be invested? It can be loaned out to private or public parties, but this merely defers the question, since capital can only be returned with interest if it has been borrowed by profit-making enterprises or governments collecting taxes from the activities of same. Profit-making enterprises are the crux. And these depend on providing goods or services that can be sold for more than it costs to produce them. But to whom can these commodities be sold? Capital temporarily frozen in the form of commodities can only realize a profit through the good offices of purchasers, who for the most part must either be consumers (if you are selling consumer goods, e.g., cars) or firms that produce for consumers (if you are selling capital goods, e.g., conveyor belts). At some equilibrium level, the ratio of profits to wages will *not* be too high to interfere with the valorization of capital. Above that level, however, profits are made at *too great* an expense to wages, with the result that consumer demand is no longer enough to secure the realization by capital of the average rate of profit. That average will then decline—as has been the secular trend across the rich countries since the '70s—even as the ratio of profits to wages remains elevated.

The commonplace profit squeeze thesis, however, argues in effect that the rate of exploitation (for all that mainstream economics would spurn the term) sank too low around 1970 and has stayed depressed ever since. The "reserve price" of labor, to use more congenial terminology—the wage beneath which labor refuses to work—is even now too high, owing presumably to an exaggerated sense of dignity among workers or the tyranny of the minimum wage. The possibility can be entertained. But when the wage share of GDP has steadily fallen across the rich countries while their overall growth rates continue to slide, the opposite possibility looks more likely: only a rising total wage bill during the '70s and after could have ensured consumer demand consistent with the maintenance of full employment—and a sustainably high rate of return. No less an authority than Kalecki,[*] in his classic essay on "The Political Aspects of Full Employment" (1943), insisted that "profits would be higher under a regime of full employment than under *laissez-faire*." He and others produced models to bear the contention out; the models are unsurprising if you consider that full employment by definition entails expanded economic activity.

There are also historical reasons for supposing that the central flaw of postwar capitalism lay in not-full-enough employment. The interpretation of the inflationary troubles of the '70s as a price spiral induced by high wages (along with high oil prices) is not the only one; in the late '70s, with inflation at its postwar worst, unemployment also ran much higher than in prior decades. In America, the Ford and Carter administrations attempted to stimulate the economy by deficit spending and tax cuts, but so long as workers were not

---

[*] The Polish economist Michał Kalecki (1899–1970) developed a "Keynesian" theory of business cycles, liquidity traps, and countercyclical spending independently of Keynes. In economics departments outside the US, he is usually given credit for this. But Kalecki's politics were Marxist.

producing a supply of goods and services commensurate with the increased monetary demand, what could the prices of existing goods and services do but rise? Another solution would have been to create new jobs, turning out new commodities, to soak up excess currency. But this could only have been achieved at the cost, unthinkable to business, of greater power for labor.

In the event, the international economy of the long down-turn ever more closely approximated a zero-sum game in which no economy's success could be purchased except at another's expense. (See Brenner's account of the seesawing fortunes of Germany, Japan, and the US.) The path toward prosperity for later-developing large economies lay in export-ing "tradeables" to the international market. In Germany and Japan, and then in China, catering to external markets won out over nurturing internal demand. Domestic wage repres-sion, usually in combination with an undervalued currency, formed the precondition of international competitiveness. Meanwhile, the old import-substitution regimes of Latin America, which focused on domestic rather than interna-tional markets, were considered discredited, despite having compiled a record of macroeconomic performance better than anything achieved by Latin America under neoliberalism.

In light of the recent recession, the limits to export-led growth now seem plain. On one hand, the entrance onto the world market of lower-cost producers in Asia threatened to undermine the hard-won position of any given rich country. (Indeed Japan has secured its continued if shaky prosperity largely through investment in other Asian economies.) On the other hand, the growth of supply in international trade has simply outrun that of demand. The telltale sign of this was always the towering current account deficits run by the US. On the strength of borrowed money and the "wealth effect" that permitted withdrawals against rising asset prices, American consumers, and their counterparts in places like the U.K. and Spain, could absorb enough of the world's exports to avert stagnation. The American situation had the neatness of tragedy or comedy: the health of the world economy would depend on the spending habits of the people most completely committed to wage restraint! (The wage share of American GDP—subtracting the top 5 percent of earners— fell from a height above 63 percent in 1969 to 52 percent and declining in 2005.) But the US role as global buyer of last resort was compromised by mass mortgage and credit card defaults and the precipitous drop, in 2008, of equity and real estate prices.

So far this has inspired no doctrinal conversion, in the economic ministries of the world, to the developmentalism favored by poorer nations during the Golden Age, but there are signs that net-exporting countries are reorienting themselves toward domestic consumption. A recent *Slate* piece by Daniel Gross takes up the theme: "Countries stung by the sudden drop-off in demand from foreign buyers have realized that they can no longer simply export their way to prosperity. China's exports fell 23 percent between August 2008 and August 2009. Smart investors are channeling resources to companies that produce domestic goods for domestic markets." Of course only a few countries like China and the US have vast enough domestic markets to pursue such a course; smaller nations in, for instance, Europe and South America would have to form "domestic" markets among themselves through bodies like the EU and Mercosur. At any rate, the success of such a strategy depends on a rising wage bill in domestic markets. And this in turn implies expanded (if not yet full) employment.

Whether the Golden Age came to an end, and whether our own leaden age has persisted, because the wage bill of the international working class ran too high or too low can't be settled here. But the illicit prestige that economists have enjoyed in recent years—a byproduct of so much forbidding mathematics, occupational arrogance, and coincidence with speculative bubbles—should not lead us to believe that the question has been answered among conferring neutral experts. Last year I had the chance to ask Nouriel Roubini—a disciplinary eclectic known for the breadth of his reading and the independence of his views, and world-famous for having predicted the financial crisis with extraordinary accuracy—if it might be that unemployment and wage stagnation on an international scale lay at the bottom of the global recession. His reply is worth quoting in full.

"Even without being Marxian," Roubini said,

> income is allocated between labor and capital. Capital has a greater marginal propensity to save out of that income, and labor has a greater marginal propensity to spend. And

it's a fine balance, because if there is too much capital accumulation and you produce too many goods, and the final demand is not there because wage earners don't have enough income, then you can be in an equilibrium of low growth. That is the big conundrum we have to think about. If you want to take the more radical view, you say wages were not growing fast enough, capital income was growing fast, and the only way you got enough final demand is by allowing people to borrow against income they didn't have. For a while, demand was sustained by equity and housing bubbles. Right now the reckoning has arrived, people have to live within their means, real wages are not growing fast enough, therefore we may be in— unless there is a change in distribution of income and wealth—a period of subpar growth. It's a possibility, a hypothesis. I wouldn't say it's for sure true. The years to come are going to test it.

Suppose that we are witnessing the end of the global imbalances that mounted so teeteringly high over the last decade, a collective folly in which one group of countries, led by the US, purchased the surplus goods of another group, led by China and Japan, with money the first group did not possess and had to borrow from the second. Neither group, at least not their corporations or governments, truly wanted anything like full employment. For the net-exporting countries, full employment would have raised wage costs and threatened competitiveness. For the net-importing countries, full employment would have triggered inflation and so undermined purchasing power and asset prices. True, the lack of full employment spelled inadequate aggregate demand across the system. But an increasingly baroque financial shell game conjured just enough demand to keep things afloat—until it didn't. Now the world's exports can no longer be purchased with phantom wages. Now the project of developing internal markets in country after country will encourage the revival of true full employment as a condition of adequate overall demand. Global prosperity will come about not through further concessions from labor, or the elimination of industrial overcapacity by widespread bankruptcy, but through the development of societies in which people can afford to consume more of what they produce, and produce more with the entire labor force at work.

There are plenty of reasons to suspect this is only a daydream, not least the veto that international finance continues to wield over the policies of any country needing to borrow money to stimulate domestic development.* But if the US is to recommit itself to full employment, the first battle will have to be over the very definition of the term. Since Milton Friedman's 1967 paper on the "natural rate of unemployment," economic orthodoxy has defined full employment along Friedmanite lines as the Non-Accelerating Inflation Rate of Unemployment, or NAIRU. This is *full employment* not as common sense would gloss it—a job for

---

* Keynes: "The whole management of the domestic economy depends upon being free to have the appropriate rate of interest without reference to the rates prevailing elsewhere in the world. Capital control is a corollary of this."

all those willing and able to work—but as just enough unemployment for wage demands not to drive up inflation. Today full employment is defined by the Bureau of Labor Statistics as 4.9 percent *unemployment.*

It's true that full employment as common sense would understand the term has often been accompanied by relatively high inflation: the example of Sweden before 1990 is handiest. And there is no denying that inflation above a certain level (about 8 percent annually, it seems) begins to harm everyone except massive debtors. Below that threshold, however, inflation can be convenient for a variety of economic actors. Workers will often accept a nominal increase in wages that is scant gain in real terms; firms are encouraged to borrow if inflation keeps real interest rates low and eases the repayment of loans; and idle capital is tempted into investment by the steady erosion of value it otherwise suffers. But—and here is the problem—financial capital refuses to tolerate otherwise acceptable levels of inflation. In recent decades, straitened avenues for profitable investment have released vast migrating swarms of "finance." Riding a bubble, and jumping off in time, has been the great ambition of this capital; disintegrating through inflation, the overriding fear. Thus the generation-long ascendancy of financial capital has expressed itself in a preference for a monetarist or Friedmanite definition of full employment, one in which the dangers of inflation have been oversold at the expense of the unemployed, wage-earners, and industry too. Even now, in what is if anything a deflationary climate, an unreasoning fear of inflation dominates public debate.

*   *   *

In 1978, Congress made it an explicit purpose of the Federal Reserve to promote full employment, as well as price stability. (The European Central Bank, by contrast, is tasked only with stabilizing prices.) The goal of full employment is inscribed in our financial system. It should now become a political demand with which to counter efforts by the Obama administration and congressional Republicans to fight mass unemployment by means of tax credits for employers. If it is not already obvious that these pitiful initiatives, not even sincere enough to qualify as wishful thinking, are knowingly inadequate to the problem they pretend to address, that will be plain enough in the months and years ahead.

A basic charter of full employment might begin with three simple articles. Article 1 would insist that the words mean what they say: full employment. Let galloping inflation retain its well-deserved stigma; a moderate level of inflation is more often than not a sign of economic health.

Article 2 would specify a living wage. The vision, popular on the right, of full employment through misery—the willingness of paupers to do anything to survive—is both an abomination and an error. Academic Keynesians have exposed the fallacies in the right's call for the reduction or abolition of the minimum wage, and their demonstrations don't need to be repeated here. The left's contribution to the debate would lie in the simple and irrefutable proposition that a mentally and physically able adult is capable of producing at least enough economic value to sustain him or her at a decent standard of living. The very existence of mass unemployment *without* mass starvation and homelessness proves that all workers can support at least themselves. In any complex economy they support more or less double their number, not to mention underwriting all war, luxury, art, and thought. No one capable of doing anything economically valuable need be a charity case in receiving a living wage.

Article 3 would stipulate the state's responsibility for achieving full employment. The most traditional object of public employment is public works of the kind associated with the Work Progress Administration. Between 1936 and 1939, the WPA spent about 2 percent of GDP per year in employing two and half million people to build over 4,000 schools and 130 hospitals, and to repair or pave 280,000 miles of road. The stimulus of the American Recovery and Reinvestment Act has been, by contrast, timorous and wasteful. According to Doug Henwood in his invaluable *Left Business Observer*:

> At most ... ARRA has "saved or created"—a spongy concept—a number of jobs equal to about 0.5 percent of total employment . . . And this has come at a cost of almost $250,000 a job! Even if you allow for a multiplier effect in employment, and assume that each of these jobs generated another half or three-quarters of a job, we're still talking well over $100,000 a job. It would have been far more efficient just to create old-style public works at, say, $40,000 a pop.

Still, the need for public works, and the capacity of the government to pay for them, are not unlimited. If private business, ordinary government administration, and public works expenditure all fail to achieve full employment, let the government sponsor workers' cooperatives producing marketable goods and services. Such cooperatives would receive startup loans from the government, but would then survive on their own income or, like other businesses, fail. Compensation would be set by the workers themselves, and any profits of enterprise likewise distributed by labor/management. If workers' co-ops can outcompete capitalist firms, then let the devil take the hindmost.* Such a program shouldn't be judged too utopian: employee stock ownership plans (ESOPs) in the US, and, more spectacularly, the successes of the recovered factory movement in post-2001 Argentina point up the viability of worker-owned enterprises within capitalism. If the capitalist dispensation were to erode firm by firm into an economy of associated producers, slowly eliminating distinctions between labor and capital and workers and management, we would have all the more reason for stripping the first quarter-century after World War II of its title as the Golden Age. The maxim *L'âge d'or était l'âge où l'or ne régnait pas* is wrong only in its past tense: the Golden Age will be when gold—or rather capital—no longer rules.

Of course today any thought of a golden future for humanity is all but stifled before utterance by ecological dread. So it should be added that full employment wouldn't win us much

---

   *   The terror inspired by the notion of a "public option" attached to health care reform always indicated the bad faith behind familiar eulogies to the marvelous competitiveness of capital by comparison with the lumbering state. If the self-description of business were accurate, it would have nothing to fear from public competition.

unless accompanied by the reduction of greenhouse gas emissions, peak oil mitigation, and the conservation of forests, topsoil, fisheries, and so on. Full employment and ecological sustainability might even complement one another, since full employment on an international scale would raise the price of raw materials and fossil energy, and in this way eventually, though not at first, encourage their conservation. And at least until the (perhaps impossible) transition to a sustainable energy regime endowed with the same transportation capacities as our own doomed fossil system, full employment would promote the localization of production by raising fuel costs. This would in turn deprive capital of some of its capacity for geographical wage arbitrage, and strengthen the hand of labor.

It is also worth pointing out that the goal of full employment doesn't entail, and shouldn't imply, either a "productivist" celebration of paid labor or the vision of society as an enormous workhouse in which all able-bodied adults spend half their waking lives on the job. The greater the number of people at work, the fewer hours each must work to achieve the same overall result. More leisure or free time, not less, would be one natural—and desirable—consequence of having more jobs.

Meanwhile, a renewed demand for full employment must insist on a literal reading of the term; a living wage; and the responsibility of the state to ensure jobs whenever business does not. Possibly to achieve true full employment where the long postwar boom only approached that condition would only revive and confirm the profit-squeeze thesis, and enforce the conclusion that full employment is as ruinous to capitalism as commonly supposed. In that case, the attenuation of profitability, at a high plane of prosperity, might lead us to recall Marx's proposition that no social order is ever overcome until all its productive capacities—surely these include those of its working people—have been fulfilled. Turning away (revolution is the word) from profitability as the index of social health, we might attain a nearly steady-state summit of civilization, and content ourselves with a slow-growing economy in which the red of socialism had been interfused with the green of sustainability. Or—a more pedestrian chance—full employment might spell nothing worse for capital than moderate inflation, with a balanced rate of exploitation securing the steady growth of wages and profits both. On this subject the last word still belongs to Kalecki: "If capitalism can adjust itself to full employment, a fundamental reform will have been incorporated in it. If not, it will show itself an outmoded system which must be scrapped."

February 2010

4

David Graeber: In the Midst of Life We Are in Debt

Most analysts divide postwar capitalism into two periods. The first extends from the late 1940s into the 1970s. The end of the second appears to have been announced by the crisis—at first a "financial" crisis, now often a "debt" crisis—that broke out in 2008. The precise boundary between the postwar eras gets drawn differently depending on which feature of the terrain is emphasized. In terms of overall growth rates, it was with the recession of 1973–74 that the surge after World War II gave way to deceleration across the wealthy world. Intellectually, Milton Friedman's Nobel Prize of 1976 signaled the shift from Keynesianism to monetarism; thereafter orthodox economics was more concerned with low inflation than full employment. Politically, the neoliberal turn began later, perhaps with Thatcher's election in 1979. At any rate, a new kind of socioeconomic arrangement—the Marxian economists Gérard Duménil and Dominique Lévy propose the name "neoliberalism under US hegemony"—emerged from the turmoil of the 1970s, and is now failing.

Writers who stress the role of debt in the story tend to see 1971 as the cusp. So it is in *Paper Promises*, a brisk digest of changes in Western monetary policy over the last few centuries by the *Economist* writer Philip Coggan, and in *Debt: The First 5,000 Years* by the anthropologist and activist David Graeber, which situates the same stretch of modern history within the vast tidal shifts, across five millennia of Eurasian history, between monetary regimes founded on precious metals and those based on "virtual credit money." In August 1971, Nixon suspended the convertibility of the US dollar into gold. Until then, foreign central banks had been entitled, under the terms of the Bretton Woods system established after World War II, to redeem dollar holdings at a rate of $35 an ounce. Whether or not this modified gold standard sponsored or merely accompanied the unprecedented expansion after 1945, it discouraged extravagance among international debtors. To sink too far into debt—in terms either of the national budget or the balance of accounts with trading partners—was to risk being sapped of gold. For this reason among others, the first postwar decades saw steeply declining ratios of national debt to GDP across advanced economies. These years were also more or less free of the great, listing trade imbalances of the current era, which allow Americans, Spaniards, or Britons to buy so much more from foreigners than they sell to them.

The debt-restraining trends of the Bretton Woods settlement were not reversed until, in the late 1960s, the US began to live—and kill—considerably beyond its immediate means, borrowing enormous sums to cover Johnson's Great Society and the Vietnam War. It was to avert a run on American reserves that Nixon first disconnected the circuit between paper and bullion. When dollar-gold convertibility was abandoned once and for all in 1973, borrowers and lenders began to ply a more insubstantial trade. In the decades since, all monetary debts have been mere "paper promises." Paper money debts, Coggan argues, being no more than titles to future slips of paper, multiply more easily than debts reckoned in fixed sums of specie, and, starting in the early 1970s, overall indebtedness has indeed grown faster than most national economies: "In the last forty years, the world has been more successful at creating claims on wealth than it has at creating wealth itself." Four decades ago, the US had a total debt burden—adding up the liabilities of government, businesses, and individuals—hardly larger than its annual output. By 2010, many countries labored under debt burdens several times the size of GDP. The American figure was approximately three to one; the British, four and a half to one. In Ireland and Iceland, total debt to output ratios had swollen to eight or ten to one on the eve of the 2008 collapse.

The new prominence of debt in rich countries—no novelty in poorer ones—has lately been matched by its political salience. In Greece, Portugal, and Spain, sovereign debt burdens have driven protesters onto the streets in the tens of thousands. They are indignant at being made to repair their governments' books through higher taxes and reduced salaries and benefits. In Chile, excessive interest rates on student loans figured among the main grievances in demonstrations throughout the southern winter. And the Occupy movement in the US—whose slogan, "We are the 99 percent," was reportedly first floated by Graeber himself—has condemned not only the maldistribution of wealth but the related vice of massive consumer debt, in the form of mortgages, student loans, and usurious interest rates on credit cards. Generally speaking, the 1 percent lends and the rest borrow.

Western politicians meanwhile excuse their policies by alluding to the national debt. Austerity is required, they say, to placate the bond market—that is, buyers of sovereign debt. The argument enjoys a popularity with elites independent of its local plausibility. Countries like the US and the U.K., able to borrow in their own currencies, have throughout the crisis auctioned new bonds at very low rates of interest— sometimes less than 2 percent—while the borrowing costs for weaker members of the eurozone have spiked to ruinous levels. Faced with a generation of collective debt servitude, many Greeks have glanced enviously at Argentina, which ten years ago undertook the largest sovereign default in history. In the 1990s, Argentina had pegged the peso to the dollar. When recession struck, the country was left with huge debts denominated in a foreign currency, and no capacity to regain the competitiveness of its exports through devaluation: a familiar predicament in Europe just now. Default, to the tune of $100 billion, was the result. All but shut out of international credit markets over the past decade, Argentina has nevertheless posted growth rates of about 8 percent a year. Post-crash Argentina, however, enjoyed advantages unknown in the eurozone: a titanic exporter of foodstuffs, it stood on the brink of a commodities boom, and also had the friendship of Hugo Chávez in Venezuela, who financed his fellow left populists in Buenos Aires on generous terms.

Whether or not class struggle is the motor of history, it rarely goes by that name. Coggan attempts to stay above the fray: "Economic history has been a war between creditors and debtors, with the nature of money as the battleground." Graeber, for his part, enlists on the side of the debtors. His extraordinary book, at once learned and freewheeling, concludes with a call for a "biblical-style jubilee"—in the Old Testament, one was declared every fifty years—to cancel outstanding consumer and government loans: "Nothing would be more important than to wipe the slate clean for everyone, mark a break with our accustomed morality, and start again." In a way, Graeber's utopian proposal resembles Coggan's anxious anticipation of the years ahead. "Borrowers," Coggan writes in his brooding introduction, "will fail to pay back their debts, either through outright default or by encouraging their governments to inflate the debt away."

Default or forgiveness, bankruptcy or jubilee: the different terms for the erasure of debts reflect a divergence of mood founded on different social positions. Individuals owe debts to private lenders and—through taxes—to governments. But, conversely, governments and corporations owe debts to individuals by way of pensions and healthcare plans, not to mention bonds. And many of the banks to which so many of us owe so much money are themselves technically insolvent: to over-lend during the bubble, they had to over-borrow. So, too, are there net-creditors (China or Germany) and net-debtors (the US or Spain) among nations. Many of the economic promises made over the last decades will not be kept; much depends on which, and whose, promises these are.

Graeber, an American who teaches anthropology at Goldsmith's College in London, is a veteran of the alterglobalization movement, which sought debt forgiveness for the Global South. Closely involved in planning the occupation of Zuccotti Park in Lower Manhattan that began in September 2011, Graeber, who describes himself as an anarchist, joined those successfully advocating a non-hierarchical or "horizontal" organization for the encampment: deliberation by consensus, no formal leadership. In the months since, the American media, content to ignore *Debt* when it first appeared (published as it was by a small press and animated by a radical politics), has hailed Graeber as the most intellectually imposing voice of Occupy. In person Graeber is brilliant, if somewhat hectic, plain-spoken, erudite, quick to indignation as to well as to laughter, and—minus the laugh— he offers much the same heady experience on the page. *Debt* is probably best considered as a long written-out lecture, informal in style, rather than as a conventional work of history, economics, or anthropology.

As the mock-heroic subtitle suggests, the scope of *Debt* is far too wide to allow a comprehensive treatment of its theme. Nor does the book offer a central analytic argument identifying the causal mechanics of social change. Partial in both senses, *Debt* aims to tear away the veil of money draped over the world and expose the credit system as so many naked human relationships, mostly violent and unjust. The colossal historical inertia behind organized domination needn't triumph—so *Debt* implies—over small groups of people converted to a dissident conception of what the members of a society "truly owe" each other.

Graeber's first proposition is that debt can't be considered apart from the history of money, when it is money that distinguishes a debt from a mere obligation or promise. Obligations are immemorial and incalculable, but until the advent of money such relations of mutual obligation evade mathematical specification. Only through money do nebulous obligations condense into numerically precise debts, which can and—according to "our accustomed morality"—must one day be paid off.

The first role of money (at least as an agent of commerce: Graeber will later discuss its truly aboriginal function) was not to grease exchange but to tabulate debts. Mesopotamian tablets dating from 3500 BC record rent, usually in the form of grain, owed by tenants of temple lands, and rations of barley due temple workers. These credits and debits may have been calculated in silver shekels, but coins hardly circulated at the time. In other words, of the three functions ascribed to money by economics textbooks—a medium of exchange, a unit of account, and a store of value—it was the second that came first. Coinage did not become widespread until several thousand years later.

Graeber insists on the historical priority of debt to exchange in order to dispel the anthropological premise of modern economics: "the myth of barter." Adam Smith supposed, as primers on economics complacently repeat, that economic life emerged from a propensity of the species to truck and barter. *The Wealth of Nations* imagines "a tribe of hunters or shepherds" among whom producers of arrowheads, tanned hides, or "little huts or moveable houses" simply swap one thing directly for another. Eventually, however, economies become too complex to function like this, and so they introduce some universal commodity—salt, cowries, or one or another precious metal—by means of which all other commodities can be exchanged. Graeber rejects this creation myth of *homo economicus* on two grounds. Not only does it mistake the origin of commercial money, which lies in credit and debt rather than exchange, it also mischaracterizes the economic behavior of earlier societies. The anthropological literature offers no evidence of barter as a central economic practice prior to money, but does furnish endless documentation of societies that distribute what we now call goods and services without drawing up accounts or expecting that such accounts, were they kept, could ever balance exactly or be closed.

The theoretical core of *Debt* is a loose schema of three types of human economic relationship. Communism (Graeber admits his use of the word "is a bit provocative"), exchange, and hierarchy don't describe distinct types of society but different "modalities" of behavior that operate to a greater or lesser degree in all societies, monetized or not. Graeber's communism, which bears a resemblance to Kropotkin's "mutual aid," covers relationships answering to Marx's dictum: to each according to his needs, from each according to his abilities. People act as communists not only towards friends and family but often towards guests, neighbors, and strangers: "What is equal on both sides is the knowledge that the other person *would* do the same for you, not that they necessarily *will*." Relationships of exchange, by contrast, entail that each party gets from the other a more or less exact equivalent to whatever it's been given. Because exchange "gives us a way to call it even: hence, to end the relationship," it takes place mostly among strangers. Hierarchy is, like communism, a mode of ongoing relationship, but between unequals. Enforced by custom, hierarchy requires that social inferiors make repeated material tribute to their betters in caste or status.

With this tripartite scheme in place, and illustrated with examples from Sudan to Greenland to medieval Europe, Graeber is ready to define the peculiarity of monetary debts. Like other market transactions, a loan is agreed to by formal equals, neither of them legally required to lend or borrow. But so long as a debt is outstanding—and any debt, being "an exchange that has not been brought to completion," extends across time—"the logic of hierarchy takes hold." Equality is restored only when repayment is made in full. The servicing of debt can meanwhile become a way to practically dominate the formally free, to exact a stream of tribute in societies without official hierarchies. The implication is that orthodox economics, by presuming exchange to be the source and circumference of economic life, misses something about both the sociohistorical environment and the political essence of debt—for relationships of hierarchy and communism both historically precede and socially encompass all apparently uncoerced and spontaneous transactions, while monetary debts often smuggle gradations of power into what look like horizontal exchanges. (An intriguing question, neglected by Graeber, is whether a large-scale credit system couldn't one day promote communism rather than hierarchy, a possibility glimpsed, or anyway named, in the literary theorist Richard Dienst's recent *Bonds of Debt*, which at one point rather vaguely imagines a future "radical politics of indebtedness" fulfilling the slogans of classical Marxism.)

But regular monetized exchanges—completed or incomplete—are a relative historical latecomer, as Graeber points out in a brace of fascinating chapters. Money, in the sense of units of abstract or general value, wasn't unknown to intimate "human economies" of village and tribe, but it didn't channel the daily flow of goods and services. So-called primitive money was instead a ritual and occasional device. Thus the "bridewealth" yielded to a woman's family by her suitor might, among the Tiv of Central Nigeria, take the form of a quantity of brass rods; or a murderer, among the Iroquois, might make reparations to his victim's family with a gift of white wampum. The inaugural use of money, then, wasn't even to record commercial debts but—in currencies of cloth or metal, whale teeth, or oxen, and sometimes human beings themselves—to betoken "debts that cannot possibly be paid."

In Graeber's book, a certain literalism about money, an unblushing faith in its capacity to determine or discover genuinely equivalent values, is the mark—or blemish—of commercial economies. The most extreme example is slavery. The buying and selling of people is an ancient practice, yet in the Atlantic slave trade Graeber sees the collision of several of his human economies with a late-model commercial one. Long before trade in human chattel, the Tiv and the Lele possessed the concepts, respectively, of "flesh-debts" and "debt pawns." A bridegroom might owe his in-laws a sister, or a man who had escaped death owe his rescuer a future son. Still, Graeber claims that the violence implied by titles in human life was, before the impact of commercial economies, more potential than actual. A Tiv without a sister for his bride's family might offer brass rods instead, while among the Lele—as in some gigantic metaphor for community—almost every man was at once the possessor of debt pawns and someone else's pawn. Neither women nor men could be bought or sold; in effect, a life had a price on it and was at the same time inalienable.

The paradox was too subtle or inconvenient for commercial economies to abide. In the seventeenth century the Aro Confederacy conspired with local rulers and European traders to impose on a portion of Africa a new commodification of human life. Debts incurred as civil penalties for the violation of (often freshly and cynically promulgated) ritual laws might be denominated in copper, but for a villager unable to scare up enough copper the next expedient might be the sale into slavery of a dependent, a pawn, or even the debtor himself. How are human economies—where "money is not a way of buying or trading human beings, but a way of expressing just how much one cannot do so"—transmogrified into slave markets? In *Debt*, it is organized violence that works the change. Only at the point of a sword, spear, or gun will a household or community accept the literal and commercial, as opposed to metaphoric and social, transitivity of human life and money.

Two main features of this discussion loom over the rest of the book. The first is an emphasis on the merely conventional nature of money, as a reflection of a social understanding that in principle could just as easily be dissolved as compacted. Commercial economies, in other words, routinely grant credit arrangements a factitious independence from social interchange, so that primary relationships seem to obtain not between human beings but between two sums of money, one loaned and the other due, while people themselves become mere bystanders to the accumulation of compound interest. The second is Graeber's argument that such a reification of monetary debts can only be maintained by force. A debt is "a promise corrupted by both math and violence." The math abstracts obligation from the fluid process of community, while the violence wielded by mafias or the state enforces the abstraction.

Already here Graeber is courting some familiar objections to the anarchist bias against distant or impersonal relationships and state monopolies on violence. Can't legal administration—as opposed to informal association—be the vehicle of justice as well as injustice? And isn't the reverse also true, so that an exclusive reliance on anarchist collectivity might offer less in the way of happiness, freedom or whatever we are finally after, than a society permitting the supervention of an armed and bureaucratized state? But these questions can be postponed until we pass through Graeber's history of debt from its ancient Near Eastern foundations to the tremors lately shaking Wall Street.

Graeber divides the history of commercial economies into five periods demarcated according to whether metallic bullion or "virtual credit money" prevailed. The periodization is approximate and the whole scheme patently heuristic, but the rough-hewn construction shelters important insights. In modern times, a gold standard, liable to low inflation or even deflation, has tended to reward creditors and punish debtors, while the reverse has been true for inflation-prone paper currency. As Keynes explained in a polemic against the "barbarous relic" of gold, deflation, by increasing the value of money, "involves a transference of wealth from the rest of the community to the rentier class and to all holders of titles to money." By the same token, the cheapening of money through inflation erodes the real value of debts and eases their repayment. Graeber doesn't dispute the general application of this rule of thumb, but at no point is he straightforwardly against bullion and in favor of credit. Metallic and virtual money can each in their own way enact the corruption of social promises into economic debts.

In the fourth millennium BC, at the dawn of the great agrarian civilizations, interest-bearing loans were widely established in Mesopotamia without the use of coins, with wares forwarded to merchants or peasants against returns from commercial expeditions or future harvests. Peasants might have to offer family members as sureties, to be collected in the event of default. By around 2400 BC, indebtedness in the Sumerian kingdom of Lagash had become insupportable, and the monarch was moved to decree history's first recorded debt cancellation, precursor to the biblical jubilee. Graeber argues this set the pattern for the virtual-money commercial economies of the time, in the Nile valley as well as the Fertile Crescent: the expansion and, through interest rates, intensification of credit relationships at length loads the peasantry with so much debt that rulers have little choice but to void outstanding obligations or risk overthrow.

Graeber's Axial Age runs from 800 BC to 600 AD, taking over Karl Jaspers's name for the epoch of the first great world religions. This age is defined by three conjoined developments: the turn to metallic money away from credit money; the emergence of the great philosophical tendencies and religions, from Zoroastrianism, Buddhism and Confucianism to Hinduism and the major monotheisms; and—arising together with these in China, India, the Near East, and the Mediterranean—the deployment of professional armies by the state.

What explains the consorting of coinage, wisdom, and war? The removal of precious metals from temples and estates and their diffusion into daily commerce in the form of coins seem to have been driven by war. Thus the first coins, appearing around 600 BC, were probably used as payment to Greek mercenaries, prized as soldiers from Egypt to the Crimea, who, far from home, would have had less use for cumbersome commodities or promissory notes that would go begging in their own country. The Axial Age launches a self-reinforcing pact of coin and sword. Payment of soldiers in precious metal encourages further plunder of neighboring lands for their bullion; conquest of these lands disrupts local economies functioning on credit and trust, as occupying powers demand that taxes and fines be paid in their own imperial coin; and the maintenance of such monetized economies requires the continued presence of the same professional armies that launched the cycle in the first place. The increased commercialization of life also breeds indebtedness and the sale of people into slavery; other slaves are war booty, put to work in mines. In Asia Minor (where Alexander's army "required half a ton of silver a day just for wages"), in Bronze Age India, and contemporaneously in China, Graeber finds much the same clanking concatenation of coinage, slavery, markets, and the state.

As for the third element of the Axial Age triad, the religious and philosophical schools, Graeber's reading won't surprise historical materialists: the new thinking was essentially a reaction to "impersonal markets, born of war, in which it was possible to treat even neighbors as if they were strangers." The daily use of metal coins opens up two chasms. First, money—as a substance that both is and is not itself, simultaneously a lump of matter and an instance of abstract value—suggests the separability of flesh and spirit. Second, it splits a more unified social sphere into an economy ruled by self-interest and an uncommodified community realm where other values may prevail. Axial Age ideas exhibit a contradictory variety: materialist philosophies might attempt to overcome dualism, while spiritual doctrines ratify it. But all are marked by "a kind of ideal division of spheres of human activity that endures to this day: on the one hand, the market, on the other, religion . . . Pure greed and pure generosity are complementary concepts; neither could really be imagined without the other." As today, worldviews might confirm or contest the status quo, and Graeber's description of China's "hundred schools" of philosophy suggests a premonition of his own politics: "Some of these movements didn't even have leaders, like the School of the Tillers, an anarchist movement of peasant intellectuals who set out to create egalitarian communities in the cracks and fissures between states."

Compared to his depiction of a bellicose and slaving Axial Age, Graeber's portrait of the long Middle Ages is far more admiring. They begin in India between 400 and 600 AD, when the Mauryan dynasty lapsed into a series of diminishingly powerful, mostly Buddhist kingdoms, and coincide with the spread of Islam in Western Eurasia, not reaching Europe until the close of the first millennium. The end of the epoch, when coins dropped out of circulation and money "retreated into virtuality," is announced by the Iberian conquest of a New World seamed with gold and silver. The effort to rehabilitate a period with a bad name is characteristic of Graeber's general iconoclasm. The Middle Ages undo "the military-coinage-slavery complex" of the Axial Age and mend the rift between economy and morality. Thus economic life falls "increasingly under the regulation of religious authorities. One result was a widespread movement to control, or even forbid, predatory lending. Another was a return, across Eurasia, to various forms of virtual credit money."

Credit arrangements organized by religious authorities, like the differential schedules of interest for separate castes in India, could still lead to steep inequality. Elsewhere, however, Confucian strictures against extraordinary profits or the Islamic prohibition of usury allowed markets to run on credit without indenturing one portion of the population to another. Graeber's account of medieval Muslim commerce has warmer words for the institution of the market than are usually heard on the left:

> By abandoning the usurious practices that had made them so obnoxious to their neighbors for untold centuries before, [merchants] were able to become—alongside religious teachers—the effective leaders of their communities . . . The spread of Islam allowed the market to become a global phenomenon . . . But the very fact that this was, in a certain way, a genuinely free market, not one created by the government and backed by its police and prisons—a world of handshake deals and paper promises backed only by the integrity of the signer—meant that it could never really become the world imagined by those who later adopted many of the same ideas and arguments: one of purely self-interested individuals vying for material advantage by any means at hand.

Notwithstanding some equivocations on the role of the state ("Markets were never entirely independent from the government. Islamic regimes did employ all the usual strategies of manipulating tax policy to encourage the growth of markets"), here is a glimpse of the anti-rentier but pro-market conception of economic life that must surely count as an intermediate necessity for radical politics today.

In *Debt*, the Age of the Great Capitalist Empires brings the apotheosis of the moneylender, after his medieval eclipse. Graeber joins a tradition of writers, going back at least to Schumpeter, who locate the origins of capitalism in the international credit system. (A separate school of thought argues that the conversion of the English peasantry into free tenants—but hardly owners—of agricultural land led to the generalizaton of wage labor.) Graeber follows Fernand Braudel in virtually identifying capitalism with consolidated finance, contrasting the "anti-market" of the monopolistic great capitals with the humbler local markets left over from the Middle Ages. What distinguishes Graeber's account, apart from its anecdotal richness (it seems, for instance, that gambling debts in Spain harried Cortéz into his assault on Tenochtitlan), is his emphasis on state violence. So the first stock markets, in Amsterdam and London, deal mostly in shares of the simultaneously military and mercantile East and West India companies, with their monopoly concessions granted by the state. Closer to home, the legalization of interest charges on consumer debt, reversing medieval bans on usury, promotes at once the spread and the criminalization of indebtedness, sometimes including—in sixteenth-century England, for example—capital penalties for default.

Capitalism not only yokes commerce and violence together after the fashion of the Axial Age; it also marks a reversion to slavery, and restores bullion to a central place. But the function of metal is no longer as simple as before. Mercantile capitalism hardly used coins within domestic economies; most American silver instead flowed to China, to be exchanged for silks and porcelain as the Chinese switched from paper money to coins. For Genoese bankers, gold and silver were the metallic pretext for a profusion of virtual money, as "the value of the bullion was loaned to the [Spanish] emperor to fund military operations, in exchange for papers entitling the bearer to interest-bearing annuities from the government." The continual inflationary discounting (in the face of uncertain repayment) of such sovereign debt—the Spanish or, later, Dutch and British precursors to capitalist paper money in general—unleashed the "price revolution" of early capitalism. Put simply, the paper money of the lenders multiplied much faster than the wages of the laborers, who often had to pay their taxes in scarce silver. (This combination of asset-price inflation for the wealthy and wage stagnation for workers is reminiscent of recent decades.) One effect was to reduce a debt-wracked peasantry to the status of a landless proletariat.

Graeber's attention to blood and treasure as the dirty fuels of accumulation is a welcome corrective to recent tales of the pristine birth of capitalism. Such stories, in keeping with the ostensible incorporeality of a financial age, tend to spiritualize our mode of production, imagining it as a spontaneous emanation of the marketplace or the belated expression—as of Athena, full-grown, from Zeus' skull—of a timeless Western rationality and individualism. Classical political economists, even at their most apologetic, knew better, and could speak in passing, as Mill did, of a system still shaped by "a distribution of property which was the result, not just of partition, or acquisition by industry, but of conquest and violence." Graeber's emphasis on metal and arms serves him less well when it comes to the persistence and evolution of the system into the latest era of world history, whose beginning he places in 1971.

For Graeber, our own time has so far been distinguished by a return to virtual money and the preservation of its value by force of American arms: "The new global currency is rooted in military power even more firmly than the old was." But, as Graeber himself shows, capitalist money has not consistently adhered to a metallic norm. Even Britain, stalwart of the gold standard, didn't adopt the measure until 1717, and an international gold standard dates only from the last third of the nineteenth century. Capitalism before our time also saw the riotous printing of paper money. And even when society-wide binges on credit money inspired chastened retreats to bullion, gold, or silver served chiefly to measure and stabilize prices rather than—through coins—to facilitate exchange. In this sense capitalist currency has not been much less virtual than Mesopotamian credit, also indexed to metal. Not only did capitalist powers typically suspend the convertibility of their paper during wartime, but even at the belle époque zenith of the gold standard, international money remained a kind of conjuring trick. Before 1914, as Coggan notes, "Britain's gold reserves rarely exceeded £40 million, a figure that was only 3 percent of the country's total money supply . . . Had foreign creditors demanded the conversion of their claims into gold, Britain could not have met the bill." After the war, and the fitful return to gold, Keynes argued that it no longer made sense to distinguish between "commodity money" and "representative money," or the metallic and the virtual. Gold, having "ceased to be a coin," had become "a much more abstract thing," with at most a vestigial part in the regulation by central banks of "managed representative money." Graeber wouldn't dispute this—he continually emphasizes that money is always a political, never a truly mineral phenomenon—but it does put in doubt the usefulness of differentiating capitalism from prior modes of production, or sorting out eras within its history, according to the role of bullion.

Graeber's stress on American imperial might in preserving contemporary monetary arrangements also creates an appearance of continuity just where he proposes a border. If state violence inaugurated and maintained capitalism before 1971, can the same factor set apart the decades since then? The anarchist identification of the state with violence risks becoming more axiomatic than analytic. Graeber describes the assembly over recent decades of a "giant machine designed, first and foremost, to destroy any sense of possible alternative futures." The inculcation of hopelessness rests on "a vast apparatus of armies, prisons, police, various forms of private security firms and police and military intelligence apparatus and propaganda engines of every conceivable variety, most of which do not attack alternatives directly so much as create a pervasive climate of fear, jingoistic conformity and simple despair." The blurring here of instruments of coercion and techniques of consent, of armies and advertisements, itself reveals the need for a more complex account of the way contemporary capitalism secures—if with diminishing success—the acquiescence of the governed and the punctual remittances of the indebted.

The most striking aspect of the current era in *Debt* is that it emerges as the rare period of virtual money that has so far failed to set up strong protections for debtors, whether in the form of bans on predatory lending or periodic jubilees: "Insofar as overarching grand cosmic institutions have been created that might be considered in any way parallel to the divine kings of the ancient Middle East or the religious authorities of the Middle Ages, they have not been created to protect debtors, but to enforce the rights of creditors." The IMF is Graeber's main example, to which the European Central Bank and the Federal Reserve could be added. The response of Western officials to the economic crisis, with its proximate cause in unsustainable consumer debt, has been to ensure that banks suffer as few losses as possible, while relying on the same indebted consumers—in their role as taxpayers—to keep the bankers whole. The Fed and now the ECB have loaned banks money at virtually no cost, encouraging those same banks to purchase government bonds paying much higher rates of interest: a direct subsidy of finance by the public, while millions sink into unemployment and bankruptcy. A far simpler and more effective monetary policy would have been for the government to print a new batch of money, distribute an equal amount to everyone, then sit back and watch as stagnant economies were stirred to life by the spending and debts were paid down and eroded by temporarily higher inflation. The inconceivability of such a policy is a mark not of any impracticability, but of the capture of governments by a financial oligarchy.

Although *Paper Promises* is essentially an extended piece of financial journalism, useful and efficient but captive to conventional wisdom, its treatment of the past 150 years nevertheless achieves a level of detail that Graeber must bypass. It's from Coggan that one gets a picture of the workings of the pre-1914 gold standard, of interwar monetary chaos, and of the fragility of Bretton Woods. Yet in discussing the nature of money as the central reality of economics, both authors at times produce something like the illusion they are trying to dispel: as if currency, whether paper or metallic, were a thing apart from the social production and contestation of value. Both writers see 1971 as a watershed. It's doubtful, however, that the abandonment of a residual gold standard was, even in monetary terms, the main event of the 1970s, or that it was decisive in bringing about the subsequent economic sea change.

The problem is more obvious in Coggan's case. His general proposition that a metallic standard of value favors the "creditor/rich class" while a regime of virtual money benefits "the debtor/poor class" is never integrated with his history of the postwar era. The first decades after World War II, before the US abandoned the gold standard, saw an inflationary erosion of the value of money; over the past generation, by contrast, the major currencies of the capitalist core, lacking any metallic basis, have nevertheless stubbornly resisted rapid inflation. In other words, the years of gold's long goodbye were less, not more, propitious for creditors than the virtual money era that followed. As Carmen Reinhart established in a paper cited by Coggan, the real rate of interest (taking inflation into account) was, from 1945 to 1980, as often negative as positive across developed economies; in any given year, a lender was as likely to be losing as gaining real wealth. If this didn't quite bring about Keynes's "euthanasia of the rentier," it did amount to the pacification of the rentier, even as profit rates reached historic heights: the main way for capitalists to beat inflation was by investing money, not by lending it. In recent decades, the situation has more or less reversed. In the 1960s the US financial sector harvested about 15 percent of domestic profits, while manufacturers took half of the total; by 2005, finance enjoyed nearly 40 percent of profits, and manufacturing less than 15 percent.

What happened around 1980 to rejuvenate the rentier and unleash the so-called financialization of the world economy? Why did inflation dramatically subside, and real interest rates surge, across several decades? It was not the quietus to gold. That had happened almost ten years before, and—if paper money were really a boon for debtors—might have been expected to produce an opposite combination of high inflation with low or negative interest rates, as for a few years it did. The decisive monetary event took place in October 1979, when Paul Volcker, chairman of the Federal Reserve, hiked interest rates to unprecedented levels, inducing a severe recession in North America and Europe as well as what came to be known as the Third World debt crisis, as the countries of the global South found that servicing their dollar-denominated debts had become vastly more expensive. The same high American interest rates drew capital to the US for the better part of two decades. This kept the dollar expensive, holding down the price of goods, while inflating the value of such assets as stocks, bonds, and real estate. Few arrangements friendlier to the wealthy could be devised. That this one took hold during a time of virtual or "fiat" money suggests that it is mainly the balance of social forces, and not any relationship to metal, that determines whether the nature of money better suits one class or another.

Money itself is a form of debt, a general claim on the social product, and undoubtedly the removal of the dollar from the gold standard permitted a tremendous expansion of debt claims: the granting of titles to the world's wealth far outpaced the actual production of wealth. Yet for most of the 1970s, labor wielded enough power to demand a growing share of those titles in the form of wages and welfare provision: hence generalized inflation. Since the late '70s, finance capital, in firmer control of most governments, has been better placed to multiply *its* claims: this too caused inflation, but of the restricted kind known as asset-price inflation.

In *The Crisis of Neoliberalism*—a work of lofty analysis and desiccated prose in the intellectual but not the literary tradition of Marx—Gérard Duménil and Dominique Lévy persuasively argue, much as David Harvey has, that neoliberalism has been less an ideological program on behalf of free markets than a "quest for high income on the part of the upper classes." Much of this high income, withdrawn against asset bubbles, has been, as Duménil and Lévy go on to show, "fictitious" in that it represented a claim on future wealth that neither had been nor was to be produced: as if one could buy apples at the store on the strength of titles to the more numerous future fruits of imaginary orchards. To put the argument a bit too simply, for Duménil and Lévy the crisis that began in 2007–8 derived most immediately from the attempt to extend to ordinary consumers, through rising home prices, a fictitious income long enjoyed by the financial classes. The scheme could hardly last. Imaginary orchards can appear more prolific than real ones only until the apples are picked.

It's tempting to believe that debt-fuelled financialization has been the succubus preying on advanced economies and draining them of vitality over the past thirty years, and surely that has been partly true. Why should the owners and managers of financial capital have bothered with increased investment in actual production? Their own incomes soared, never mind that the system's trajectory began to sink. Yet to dwell on Volcker's "financial coup" of 1979 as the central development of the decade, or to consider financialization apart from production, would be another way of conceding to money an autonomy it doesn't possess, in either virtual or metallic form. There is good reason to doubt whether financialization and runaway indebtedness caused the system-wide deceleration since the 1970s, or merely concealed and at length compounded it. Orthodox economics over the last generation has neglected issues of capitalist dynamics, so it has fallen mainly to Marxian thinkers to search for the causes of ebbing growth. Robert

Brenner has adduced overcapacity in international manufacturing as the trigger of a systemic slowdown starting in 1973. Others have pointed to "the rising organic composition of capital" or—a related phenomenon—the dwindling economic importance of productivity gains in manufacturing, amid a growing preponderance of services. Graeber and Coggan don't discuss these arguments, but add to them an awareness—another product of the 1970s—of ecological checks on growth. For Coggan, the great looming threat is a permanent increase in energy costs, making future "gains in overall productivity" difficult or impossible. For Graeber, environmental limits more generally supply the main reason to believe that capitalism, as "an engine of perpetual growth . . . on a finite planet," will no longer exist "in a generation or so."

A stationary state of growthlessness, or even a situation in which per capita GDP stagnated across the globe, would only sharpen the conflict between creditors and debtors that has come into relief since 2008. If the loaning of money at interest, stigmatized as usury during the Middle Ages, has seemed a more tolerable practice during much of the history of capitalism, its acceptance has been purchased through growth: increased income for rentiers didn't necessarily imply a corresponding decrease for everyone else, only a share in the common expansion. The more nearly property relations approach a zero-sum game, the less we will be able to distinguish between what Adam Smith called productive and consumptive loans, the former contributing to the borrower's prosperity and the latter merely draining it. Positive real interest rates per se will come to seem consumptive or parasitic, a straightforward transfer of wealth from debtor to creditor. It's not inconceivable that financial rents could grow even as the economy stalls, with the subjects of capitalism submitting to an age of declining standards of living, as occurred in much of Europe during the eighteenth century. But other outcomes are possible, and more easily imagined than even a year ago, thanks to the energies of protesters round the world. Graeber's question for activists might also be taken by ruling elites as a warning: "Will a return to virtual money lead to . . . the creation of larger structures limiting the depredations of creditors?"

Most immediately, the question concerns the sado-mone-tarism, as it's been called, of the ECB. Peripheral Europe needs higher inflation, and soon, in order to shed debt and to regain a degree of competitiveness that probably can't be achieved, even at enormous human cost, through the simple reduction of wages. The Spanish cartoonist El Roto has summarized the logic of European politicians: "If the currency can't be devalued, it will have to be the people." The program has been a debacle even on its own terms, as the increasing debt burden and interest rates of Spain and other countries testify. Unless the euro—a virtual currency as inflexible, to date, as any golden fetters—is devalued, it will be hard for the EU, which has a larger economy than the US, to escape the consequences foreseen by Nouriel Roubini: "Without a much easier monetary policy . . . more eurozone countries will be forced to restructure their debts"—in other words, partly default—"and eventually some will decide to exit the monetary union." It was with the Continental crisis in mind that Paul Krugman recently voiced a thought usually confined to the radical press: "I'm really starting to think that we're heading for a crack-up of the whole system."

The prospect of systemic crack-up makes it urgent for new movements of the left to imagine what "larger structures" might govern the credit system of a society retaining its complexity and scale even as it demotes bankers to the level of ordinary citizens. Some readers of *Debt* have surmised that Graeber opposes all forms of impersonal economic relationship, on the basis of his warm accounts of neighborly credit relations or the Islamic bazaar with its "handshake deals," as well as his denunciation of a credit system, articulated through laws and defended by violence, that exempts debt obligations and the value of money from the sort of continuous revision typical of humane dealings among equals. In response, Graeber has said that he is not "against impersonal relations, or all impersonal exchange relations," which must in some degree characterize "any complex society." There is no reason to doubt him. Yet the spirit of the Occupy movement has so far been defined by what Graeber, in *Direct Action: An Ethnography* (2009), described as the—mainly anarchist—theory and practice of "direct action," or what is now often called "prefigurative politics." In this ethos, "means and ends become, effectively, indistinguishable; a way of actively engaging with the world to bring about change, in which the form of the action . . . is itself a model for the change one wishes to bring about."

The political suggestiveness of spontaneous self-organization—of protests, assemblies, and encampments—can't be denied. These practices have reminded thousands of activists that society itself, all appearances to the contrary, is the active creation of its constituents. But the stress on direct action and face-to-face assembly has also threatened to stifle, rather than inspire, a developed program for the left, as if the impersonal institutions of money, banking, and government had been too badly tainted by long collusion with oppression to be salvaged. Yet, assuming that we aren't about to see a swift unraveling of the contemporary world, knit together largely out of long-distance relations among strangers, into a far lower degree of complexity, the left will need to imagine and propose credit systems and monetary authorities that can prize apart debt and hierarchy, exchange and inequality. Money, and therefore debt, is always an abstraction. But justice too can be abstract, and there is no reason in principle why money and debt must serve injustice rather than justice. So long as we still resort to markets and banks, the words of (the socialist) George Bernard Shaw are worth keeping in mind:

> The universal regard for money is the one hopeful fact in our civilization . . . It is only when it is cheapened to worthlessness for some, and made impossibly dear to others, that it becomes a curse . . . Money is the counter that enables life to be distributed socially . . . The first duty of every citizen is to insist on having money on reasonable terms.

April 2012

5

Slavoj Žižek: The Unbearable Lightness of "Communism"

Marxism has tended to be, since the first collaborations of Marx and Engels, a thorough critique of capitalist society from the standpoint of a far less developed concept of socialism or communism. In this sense, its premise is a utopian conclusion never yet demonstrated: namely, that there can be a better form of modern society, based on a different regime of property, than one dominated by the accumulation of private capital. No one can in fairness require a detailed picture of this future condition, but the vision has to enjoy some minimum plausibility. Otherwise, only a description of capitalism can be offered, and some suggestions for reform, but no fundamental criticism.

Since the 1970s—and especially since 1991—perhaps the greatest challenge for Marxism has been to keep alive the belief in the possibility of a superior future society. The belief was trampled almost to extinction by miscarried Third World revolutions, capitalist transformation in China, the capitulations of European socialist parties, Soviet collapse, and the ostensible triumph of liberal capitalism. The skepticism that replaced it was twofold. The would-be revolutionary left seemed to possess neither a serious strategy for the conquest of power nor a program to implement should power be won. In this context, the maximalism of the left at its high-water marks could only ebb into a kind of survivalist minimalism. The pith of minimalism lay in the alter-globalization slogan: "Another world is possible." Its most eloquent expression may have been Fredric Jameson's book on Utopia, *Archaeologies of the Future* (2005), which sought to preserve the concept of a break with capitalism in conditions under which neither the bridge across the chasm nor the institutions lying on the other side could be imagined.

These are the reduced circumstances in which the Slovenian philosopher Slavoj Žižek has been, for at least the past dozen years or so, the world's best-known Marxist thinker. With graphomaniacal productivity and postmodern range, Žižek writes mainly about contemporary ideology and culture in the broad sense that covers everything from an animated Hollywood blockbuster such as *Kung Fu Panda* to the forbidding ontology of Alain Badiou. Corrugated with dialectical reversals and seeming at times to consist exclusively of digressions, Žižek's writing is often described, with some justice, as elusive. Even so, his basic analysis of the end-of-history ideology that swept the world after 1991 has been simple enough.

Žižek ventriloquized the mindset in *First as Tragedy, Then as Farce* (2009), one of his many entertaining, funny, and shamelessly repetitive books: "Capitalism is a system which has no philosophical pretensions . . . The only thing it says is: 'Well, this functions.' And if people want to live better, it is preferable to use this mechanism, because it functions." As he went on to argue in his own voice, "The very notion of capitalism as a neutral social mechanism is ideology (even utopian ideology) at its purest." In fact, neoliberal "post-ideology" resembled nothing so much as a caricature of Marxist historical determinism. It merely substituted liberal capitalism for communism in claiming that here we beheld the final form of human society, as legitimated by science—in this case, sociobiology and neoclassical economics—and as certified on the proving ground of history.

This view was often declared after the Cold War in a triumphalist spirit. Lately, with the outbreak, still uncontained, of the worst economic crisis since the 1930s, it has persisted in a more resigned key. In his latest book, Žižek quotes David Simon, creator, in the television epic *The Wire*, of as damning a portrait of class-riven America as any Marxist could wish for: "I accept that [capitalism] is the only viable way to generate wealth on a wide scale."

Žižek not only rejects this nearly unanimous conclusion but discerns in unexpected places—whether in the chauvinist eruptions of the political right or the low-grade commercial output of US cinema—the abiding wish, however disfigured and denied, for a "radical emancipatory politics." In recent years, Žižek's name for such a politics has been simply "communism." He has carried out this dual operation—against the supposed necessity of capitalism, in favor of the renewed possibility of communism—by invoking a remarkable roster of thinkers. Hegelian in philosophy, Marxist in economics, Leninist in politics, and an exponent of Jacques Lacan's particularly baroque strain of psychoanalysis, Žižek combined these ways of thinking at a time when all of them separately, let alone together, had fallen into disrepute. He knew the reaction this courted, as can be seen in a line from *In Defense of Lost Causes* (2008): "What should have been dead, disposed of, thoroughly discredited, is returning with a vengeance." Nor did this foul-mouthed wise guy, with an Eastern bloc accent out of Central Casting, baiting his detractors with talk of "good old Soviet times" and plucking at his black T-shirt with Tourettic insistence, make himself much more presentable to conventional opinion as a personality.

For many fellow leftists, it has been both a winning performance and a vexing one. Žižek isn't exactly to blame for his press, much less for the failure of the media to pay similar attention to other left-wing thinkers. Even so, his intellectual celebrity has seemed a symptom of the very intellectual impasse he has diagnosed. A ruthless criticism of capitalism, it turned out, could still be contemplated outside the academy—but only on condition that it appear as the work of a jester or provocateur. In this way, the figure of Žižek seemed to represent, encouragingly, the lifting of the post–Cold War embargo on radical thought and at the same time, discouragingly, its reimposition.

A similar ambiguity attaches to his new book, *The Year of Dreaming Dangerously*, a brief consideration of several of the revolts and convulsions of 2011, from the Arab Spring and Anders Behring Breivik's massacre in Norway to the London riots and Occupy Wall Street in the US. Did last year's dreams, with their conscious or unconscious emancipatory content, pose more of a danger to contemporary capitalism or to the dreamers themselves? In other words, did they prefigure a revolutionary challenge to the system or merely demonstrate that such an awakening remains all but inconceivable?

The book begins with Žižek's general presentation of a capitalism marked by "the long-term trend of shifting from profits to rents," "the much stronger structural role of unemployment," and the rise of a ruling class defined more by high salaries than direct capital income. Only the last of these features, however, is integrated into Žižek's explanation of political rebellion: some but not all protesters are recent graduates angry that a college degree no longer assures them a good salary. More relevant to the rest of *The Year of Dreaming Dangerously* is Žižek's contention that capitalism can't be reformed. He disdains the idea, characteristic of "the archetypal left-liberal European moron," that we need "a new political party that will return to the good old principles" and "regulate the banks and control financial excesses, guarantee free universal health care and education, etc, etc."

He proceeds to examine last year's rebellions not chronologically but in order, it seems, of increasing approximation to his own politics. For Žižek, the xenophobic Breivik's intellectual error (not to speak of his obvious moral catastrophe) is to misunderstand his own ideology: genuine fidelity to Europe's heritage of Christian universalism would seek to redeem, for Muslim immigrants as well as all others, the "legacy of radical and universal emancipation." Next, Žižek discusses the London riots. These illustrate not an inversion of universalism but a post-ideology devoid of transpersonal meaning; looters were merely, like other capitalist subjects, grabbing what they could. "One danger," Žižek writes, "is that religion will come to fill this void and restore meaning." Precisely this danger has already been realized in much of the Muslim world. Yet, in Žižek's account, the popular overthrow of Arab autocracies, even when couched in Islamist terms, contained a "radically emancipatory core" to which the secular left should remain "unconditionally faithful."

Finally, in a chapter that revises a talk given before the Occupy encampment in Lower Manhattan, Žižek explains something of what he takes radical emancipation to mean. He praises Occupy for "two basic insights." The first is that the principal political problem is capitalism "as such, not any particular corrupt form of it." The second is that "the contemporary form of representative multiparty democracy" can't address the problem; therefore, "democracy has to be reinvented." My sense, as a participant in several Occupy demonstrations and one of last's years affiliated working groups, is that disenchantment with representative democracy, at least in its American travesty, does pervade the movement. The belief that capitalism can and should be surmounted, on the other hand, is hardly unknown among Occupiers but doesn't seem general either.

Žižek sees in various popular discontents the chauvinist misprision, the consumerist absence, the communalist disguise, or the anti-capitalist incipience of his own politics. Radical politics at its most basic consists of two elements: strategy and program, or how to get power and what to do with it. Žižek's program is straightforward: the replacement of capitalism by communism. It's not necessary to disclaim this ambition, however, to see that his concept of capitalism is inadequately specified and his notion of communism barely articulated at all.

In his brief against reformism, Žižek scorns the idea that capitalism can be regulated "so that it serves the larger goals of global welfare and justice . . . accepting that markets have their own demands which should be respected." This suggests that he has confused the existence of markets with that of capitalism. The same goes for Žižek's rudimentary positive notion of communism. In *Living in the End Times* (2010), he describes a future society in which the "exchange of products" would give way to "a direct social exchange of activities." This seems to imply that individuals would no longer come by goods and services through market exchange but instead in some immediate "social" way, obviating the use of money.

Markets long predate capitalism. Capitalism is better understood as designating a society that subordinates all processes—notably the metabolism between humanity and nature, the production and distribution of goods and services, the function and composition of government, and, of course, market exchange—to the private accumulation of capital. As for communism, perhaps it goes without saying, since Žižek doesn't say so, that it means eliminating private capital on any large scale and realizing the Marxist goal of common ownership of the means of production. Yet would productive enterprises be owned by those who worked for them or by society at large—or somehow jointly between the two groups? Žižek doesn't ask, let alone answer, such questions.

Imagine, in any case, a society whose productive assets are, in one way or another, the property, as Marx said, of "the associated producers." Such a society might also entail, let's say, strict depletion quotas for both renewable and non-renewable natural resources; welfare guarantees not only for workers but for people too young, old, or ill to work; and democratic bodies, from the level of the enterprise and locality up to that of the state, wherever it hadn't withered away. These institutions might or might not be complemented by the market. For now, however, to rule markets out of any desirable future while saying next to nothing else about its institutional complexion is to reproduce the same intellectual blockage that Žižek and others ascribe to a capitalism that simply can't imagine how another kind of society might "function."

In *The Year of Dreaming Dangerously*, even the "direct exchange of activities" has vanished. Here Žižek counsels refusing capitalism from the point of view of "a communism *absconditus*" without worldly instantiation or conceptual content. He defends this featureless vision by warning, with compact incoherence, against "the temptation of determinist planning": determinism refers to inevitability, while planning implies voluntarism. Yet it requires no creed of either historical predestination or revolutionary infallibility to hazard an idea, presumably subject to revision both before and after the rupture with capitalism, of a better society. Whether such a hypothesis is called communist is a secondary question; as the poet (and revolutionary) John Milton put it in another context: "The meaning, not the name I call." At the moment, Žižek's communism is a heavy name very light on meaning.

His strategic notions, meanwhile, are various and incompatible. At times, as in his advice to Occupy, he seems to advocate the accomplishment of revolution through democracy, though he rejects parliamentary democracy for a "reinvented" kind otherwise undescribed. More often he favors a sort of Leninist quietism, according to which "those who refuse to change anything are effectively the agents of true change": withdrawal from the system will speed its collapse. Yet he allows that "a strategically well-placed, precise, 'moderate' demand can trigger a global transformation." The options at least display Žižek's dialectical facility. Apparent passivity can be the highest form of activity; then again, moderation can have immoderate effects.

Despite this last caveat, Žižek is most often and energetically an enemy of reform. The experience of western societies since World War II suggests, however, that the old opposition between reformism and revolution is no longer useful. The heyday of the welfare state was accompanied, after all, by far more worker and student radicalization than the era of neoliberalism that followed it, which demoralized radicals and reformers alike. Projects of reform, in other words, have tended to nourish hopes of revolution and vice versa. In present circumstances, the achievement of reforms might well clear, rather than bar, the way to a new society, not to mention relieving some of the human misery to be endured before the advent of the communist millennium. If, on the other hand, the system were to prove incapable of incorporating any serious reforms, this would demonstrate the need for revolution that Žižek merely asserts.

This perspective, in which reform and revolution are allied, can no doubt be intelligently contested. But the time is past for the left to content itself with the blank proposition that another world is possible. What traits, other than its otherness, would such a world possess? As liberal capitalism saps its ecological foundations, defaults on its economic promises, and forfeits its political legitimacy, another world is becoming inevitable. Which one do we want? And can we make this one into that one before it's too late?

Žižek's work at its best has shown why those questions have been so difficult even to formulate in "the desert of post-ideology." But his latest book does not interrupt the prospect of the lone and level sands.

September 2012

6

Boris Groys: Aesthetics of Utopia

Marxism has thrived as a way of thinking about art and literature, especially at times—the 1920s or the 1990s—when Marxist economic and political thinking has gone into retreat. The headwaters of the stream lie in *The German Ideology* (1846), where it seems mainly an oversight that Marx and Engels don't name art and literature, as they do religion, metaphysics, and morality, as "forms of consciousness" to be stripped of their "semblance of independence." A historical materialist aesthetics sees in art the distorted reflection of social relations past, present, and emerging. The result has often been a somewhat paradoxical model of art-making, in which the deliberate creations of the artist passively transmit unsuspected historical meaning. So in a middlebrow survey like Arnold Hauser's *Social History of Art* (1951), Balzac could appear, in spite of his titanic energies and avowed royalism, as a cat's paw of historical progress, "a revolutionary writer without wanting to be" whose "real sympathies make him an ally of rebels and nihilists." And the Marxist emphasis on the basic passivity of the artist, as a sort of crossroads of historical traffic, could be greatest where the account of art was subtlest, as in Theodor Adorno.

A broadly historical materialist approach has united so many interesting critics of the past hundred years that its fruitfulness for considering art produced under capitalism can't be denied. It has been less clear to what extent socialist theories of art could also serve as theories of *socialist* art. In practice, discussions of work by radicals in capitalist societies or by cultural revolutionaries in socialist ones have succumbed too easily to the idealism that historical materialism sought to overturn, as if the conscious politics of an Eisenstein, a Brecht, or a Paul Robeson could secure the meaning of his art. Critics have been more bleakly faithful both to materialist philosophy and to any future class-free utopia when they have considered all would-be revolutionary art as itself marked by the contradictions of class society (including socialism, which in classical Marxism is not the absence of social classes but the process of their dissolution). The Marxist critic might therefore prefer ostensibly apolitical work in which these contradictions rage untreated.

Adorno held a position like this. His posthumous *Aesthetic Theory* (1970) can be taken as the summit, with a corresponding barrenness and magnificence, of a Marxist aesthetics stressing the artist's receptivity rather than activism. Far from imagining a revolutionary popular art, as Brecht and Walter Benjamin had in different ways done in the 1930s, Adorno elaborated an aesthetics of suffering, in the senses both of passivity and pain: "Authentic works are those that surrender themselves to the historical substance of the age without reservation"; for the audience, "specifically aesthetic experience" requires "self-abandonment to artworks." As for the substance of history disclosed by true art, it is little short of agony. Adorno meant to dedicate *Aesthetic Theory* to Beckett, and the few other modernists he singles out for praise (Kafka, Schoenberg, and Celan among them) give off some of the same feeling of emotional irremediability and formal intransigence. Nor did Adorno craft a waiver for artists in self-described socialist societies, which were simply another department of "administered life." East or West, all but a handful of artworks supplied only another dose of compliance and regimentation.

Adorno is worth keeping in mind while reading Boris Groys, who is one of the more interesting philosophical—he would say antiphilosophical—writers on art today. Groys never discusses Adorno, a striking omission in light of his temper and range: *Introduction to Antiphilosophy*, Groys's latest book in English, contains essays on Kierkegaard, Heidegger, Kojève, Derrida, and Walter Benjamin. Groys, like Adorno, possesses firm if abstract radical commitments and is a writer of relentlessly dialectical sentences in German. Otherwise they represent two poles of radical aesthetics. Adorno's approach was historical materialist or Marxist yet anti-communist (at least where official Communist parties were concerned). Groys, by contrast, is more idealist in his belief that the radical artist can consciously understand and deliber-ately convey the meaning of his work—one reason, perhaps, why Groys has said he isn't a Marxist—and yet more philo-communist. His recent *Communist Postscript* (2009) joins the efforts of other contemporary thinkers, notably Slavoj Žižek and Alain Badiou, to revive communism as the rallying cry of the left.

The differences go further. Where Adorno insisted on the artist's deep passivity and independence from politics, Groys declares the artistic impulse identical to the will to power and advocates an "art functioning as political propaganda." And where Adorno's stringent conception of true art narrowed modern instances down to a few forbidding exempla, Groys's idea of art is extraordinarily expansive: he is especially attracted to art projects that efface the boundary between art and life, and has a puckish admiration for the "life-building" efforts of Soviet art.

Few later writers have shared Adorno's anhedonia or snobbish tastes; today, leftist critics are happy to discuss the political symptomatology of Hollywood blockbusters or the shellacked sexuality of pop divas. But a sense that the interest of art derives above all from its unconscious embodiment of history is widespread among academic critics, most of whom share with the general public an aversion to expressly political work. As for work by artists with obvious progressive allegiances, the usual approach is to congratulate them for raising political questions but to fight shy of definite answers. In *Art Power* (2008), Groys mocks the solemn ideological vagueness of so many academic essays, exhibition catalogues, and wall paragraphs: "The work is 'charged with tension,' 'critical' (without any indication of how or why); the artist 'deconstructs social codes,' 'puts our habitual way of seeing into question.'" Such language resembles a debased form of Adorno's aesthetics: art exposes the contradictions of capitalism but leaves them to future history to work out. Apparently a summons to politics, it is in effect an evasion. Frustration with the political nugacity of the progressive-minded art world is the background to Groys's strenuous emphasis on the "direct connection between the will to power and the artistic will." At the heart of his work is a desire for contemporary art and criticism to somehow give up the autonomy of the royal fool—whose expressive freedom derives from practical superfluousness—for something more like the autonomy of the ruler, free because in command.

Born to Russian parents in Berlin in 1947, Groys grew up and was educated in Leningrad; at college he studied mathematical logic and linguistics. In 1981 he emigrated to Münster in West Germany, where he earned a PhD in philosophy. Today he teaches art theory in Karlsruhe and New York City. This unusual itinerary has been recapitulated by Groys's intellectual trajectory and shows itself in a distinctive sensibility. After concentrating on Soviet art in *The Total Art of Stalin* (1989), he has mainly written discrete essays in which he looks, with Eastern eyes, at Western art and philosophy. *Art Power* gathers pieces on the contemporary art world—on curating, the digitization of imagery, "iconoclastic strategies in film," and so on—together with backward glances at Nazi art and socialist realism. *Introduction to Antiphilosophy* discusses a dozen or so thinkers—most of them Western European, most of them unsystematic—from Kierkegaard onwards. Only in *The Communist Postscript*, a short consideration of the relationship of communism to philosophy, does

Groys return to the USSR, making a new case for a kind of ideally existing Stalinism. Indeed the rare notes of romance struck in the otherwise unemotional register of his prose are elicited by the idea (an idiosyncratic one) of the communism he knew in his youth, and by the Muscovite *sots* (the name a disrespectfully ambiguous allusion to socialist realism) and conceptual art scene of the 1970s and '80s with which he was personally connected. His continual making and unmaking of conceptual unities and oppositions belongs to a German dialectical tradition. Yet there is no Hegelian (or Adornian) heaviness in someone who can write, "And so, the answer to the question: 'How should we conceive the apocalypse?' has to be: 'Just don't think about it!'"

Groys's many provocative formulations smack of an international art scene, centered on New York, in which flippancy and militancy can be hard to distinguish. The big question is how seriously he means to be taken, and how seriously he can be taken. The publication of *The Communist Postscript* as a little red book in Verso's Pocket Communism series is enough to suggest that Groys's tonal fluttering between clever complacency and forthright provocation, joke and dare, is not his alone on today's left.

His most substantial book, *The Total Art of Stalinism*, makes a novel argument about an episode of modern art that in most other accounts is either overlooked or moralistically dismissed. In the usual story, Stalin betrayed the Soviet revolution in the arts by imposing on artists a regime of servile kitsch. After the avant-garde flowering before and after

1917—Malevich and Lissitzky's Suprematism in painting, Eisenstein and Vertov's collectivist filmmaking, Klebnikov's "transrational" and Mayakovski's surrealist poetry— so-called socialist realism became the official program of Soviet art, now charged with "the depiction of life in its revolutionary development." This closed an era of proliferating movements, manifestos, and formal experiments; and Stalin's persecution of avant-gardists ranged from harassment to murder. Groys denies none of this. But for him Stalinism succeeds the avant-garde just as a guest accepts an invitation. Far from betraying the avant-garde, Stalin merely scuttled a transitional movement in order to fulfill on the grandest scale that movement's goal of unifying art and politics. Much of the classical avant-garde, Russian and otherwise, had after all demanded, in reaction against the sterile autonomy of *l'art pour l'art*, "that art move from representing to transforming the world": "Under Stalin the dream of the avant-garde was in fact fulfilled and the life of a society was organized in monolithic artistic forms." These forms, Groys concedes, were "of course not those the avant-garde itself had favored." Throughout he writes about Stalinist cultural policy with a hair-raising mixture of political neutrality and aesthetic appreciation.

The Total Art of Stalinism mounts a sort of triptych: the post-revolutionary avant-garde; then Stalinism; then what Groys calls Soviet "postutopianism." The brief, happy career of the avant-garde ended on April 23, 1932, when a decree of the Central Committee disbanded independent artistic groups and conscripted all "creative workers" into unitary professional unions of writers, painters, architects, and so on. Groys, who pays little attention to literature and film and virtually none to music, dwells particularly on Malevich, whose abstract canvas *Black Square*, as Groys sees it, abolishes the cultural past so that a demiurgic unity of artist, engineer, and politician may sweep into the resulting void. Not that Groys evokes the work of Malevich or other artists in detail; an art theorist with a limited plastic sensibility, he is interested mainly in art's ideological charge. Malevich once described the state as "an apparatus by which the nervous systems of its inhabitants are regulated," and for Groys the goal of the Soviet avant-garde was for artists to gain "absolute power over the world."

If the avant-garde was unknowingly daydreaming of Stalin, then Stalinist socialist realism can no longer be considered a case of cultural regression marked by the rehabilitation of mediocre popular forms and the truncation of modernist experiment. Expanded to its proper dimensions, the concept of the avant-garde includes Stalinist "total art" as its next and, so far, final embodiment. The Soviet Union, as a new kind of society chartered not only to "provide greater economic security" but also "in perhaps even greater measure meant to be beautiful," could answer to aesthetic criteria in a way that chaotic capitalist societies in thrall to the profit motive could not. Groys summarizes, apparently with approval, a critic writing in 1949 in the "ultraofficious" journal *Iskusstvo* (*Art*): "In different forms adequate to the age, Soviet socialist realism preserved the vital modernist life-building impulses that [Western] modernism itself lost long ago, when it entered the academies and prostituted itself to its arch-enemy, the philistine consumer."

Groys presents the formal staidness of socialist realism—the forced retreat from abstraction in painting, for example—as a paradoxical sign of its true vanguardism. "The radicalism of Stalinism is most apparent in the fact that it was prepared to exploit the previous forms of life and culture," whereas the avant-garde had "respected the heritage to such an extent . . . that they would rather destroy" than preserve it. What remaining need, in other words, for modern artists to *make it new* when a historically original society guarantees the novelty of all it contains? Besides, modernist representational dilemmas tended to fade away as the USSR turned to more projective forms: "Just as the avant-garde had demanded, architecture and monumental art now moved to the center of Stalinist culture."

The third panel of the book's triptych deals with Soviet art after Stalin. After Khrushchev repudiated what he called a personality cult in 1956, Soviet citizens could acknowledge that Stalin's artistic career had also entailed, as Groys says, "a chain of demoralizing atrocities." These enormities (which Groys, who in an afterword to the 2010 edition of *The Total Art of Stalinism* says he "did not want to write another body-count book," neither discusses nor disputes) don't lead him to disqualify Stalinism as an achieved utopia of total art: he has claimed it only as a singular, not a beautiful, instance of the form. But with the recognition that utopia overlay a dungeon, Soviet art couldn't go on as before. One response, in fiction by the so-called village writers, was a retreat from socialist realism to narratives wistful for "traditional Russian values." This nostalgic current found more favor with the apparat than did *sots*, and it is this "unofficial or semi-official" variety of post-Stalinist art that Groys himself admires.

Groys's postutopians—"Stalin's best pupils"—have learned the lesson of art's necessary entanglement with politics. Yet here he shifts the emphasis from Stalinism's effective wielding of art power to abstract meditations on "the aesthetico-political will to power" of artists who lacked either a mass audience or a receptive ear in the Politburo. Groys remains an associate of Vitaly Komar and Alexsander Melamid, an artist duo who in the late 1970s moved from Moscow to New York, and in the chapter on postutopianism they assume the central role earlier accorded Malevich, then Stalin. Komar and Melamid's illustrated parable *A. Ziablov* (1973) parodies the recruitment of prerevolutionary artists into the socialist realist pantheon: Ziablov—a fictional serf who anticipates abstraction in painting—becomes, in the duo's sarcastic officialese, "a lodestar to all representatives of the creative intelligentsia seeking to achieve a typical reflection of reality in its revolutionary development." A local moral could be drawn from this about Stalinism's capricious canonizations and excommunications of artists.

But Groys has a more universal case to make. Equipped with "the fundamental insight that all art represents power," Komar and Melamid appropriately give up "the search for a form of art that can resist power, because they regard such a quest as itself a manifestation of the will to power." Groys discusses (but, typically, doesn't describe) Komar and

Melamid's sardonically sumptuous oil painting *Yalta Conference* (1984): Stalin in military uniform and Spielberg's homesick alien E.T., dressed in FDR's suit and overcoat, sit together, their hands and faces gleaming like rose gold against the Venetian murk of the background, while Adolf Hitler looms behind them from the parted slit of a red Turkish tent and, undetected by the figureheads of state socialism and Hollywood capitalism, places an index finger to his moustache in a gesture of conspiratorial secret-keeping with the viewer. "The figures of Stalin and E.T.," Groys writes, "which symbolize the utopian spirit dominating both empires, reveal their unity with the national-socialist utopia of vanquished Germany."

Groys is a provocateur and the value of his work lies in its capacity to unsettle rather than convince. Despite encouraging critics of Soviet art to ground their findings in "attentive study," *The Total Art of Stalinism* is light on documentation and empirically dubious. There is good evidence, whatever Groys says, that Soviet artists before 1932 were more often preoccupied by pictorial questions than by the artist's ideal political role. Just as questionable is his presentation of Stalinism in the arts as a top-down phenomenon, without populist origins: "Socialist realism did not seek to be liked by the masses—it wanted to create masses it could like." The neat formulation contradicts Vladimir Paperny's classic *Architecture in the Age of Stalin: Culture Two* (2002), which describes how socialist realism emerged from the Soviet people as much it was imposed on them. And there is no reason to believe that Stalin chiefly thought of himself as an artist; his pretensions to being a first-rank Marxist theoretician, on the other hand, are unmistakable. Finally, why accept Stalinism as a realized utopia, however dire, when Stalinism itself—in line, to this extent, with classical Marxism—considered the Soviet Union a socialist and therefore transitional society, where no final communism had yet appeared?

Logically, too, Groys is prone to shortcuts to nowhere. One of his major difficulties lies in distinguishing Soviet postutopianism—he praises it above all other art of the last four decades—from the Western "anti-utopianism" he rejects. The apparent blank irony of *sots* art, whereby Stalin can be likened to both E.T. and Hitler, has made it seem a Soviet counterpart to pop art, which could treat Marilyn, Mao, and Coca-Cola as interchangeable icons. Among leading *sots* or postutopian themes, Groys identifies the complicity of culture with power; the inherently ideological character of experience; and the basic fictionality of all narratives. Each of these is also a basic article of the postmodernism he calls antiutopian. He resolves the problem by convicting the postmodern Westerners of a "neutralizing and transideological"—thus futile—attempt to disclose a world of teeming difference irreducible to universal projects or stories. "Russian postutopianism does not make this mistake" because it recognizes all campaigns against utopianism or metanarratives as so many instances of the totalizing ideologies the postmodernists would refuse. "To summarize the distinction it might be stated that Eastern postutopianism is not a thinking of 'difference' or the 'other' but a thinking of indifference." The question is whether this indifferentism—a flat principle, clearly Groys's own, of the inescapability of politics for all art—itself makes for an important distinction between late Soviet and contemporary capitalist art.

The Total Art of Stalinism retains its interest today because of Groys's audacious effort to break the post–Cold War taboo on utopias by welcoming the very accusation—*Stalinist!*—most effective in maintaining that taboo. Yet by the end of the book, he has inflated the notions of utopia (some version of which all aesthetics and ideologies are said to imply) and art-making (which under Stalin could extend to all activities of the state) to such dimensions that they lose as concepts the sharpness still clinging to them as rhetoric. For just as libido or eros could be said to be the taproot of all sexuality but not to be sexuality itself, merely saying that all art draws upon some universal reservoir of desire that may as well be called utopian is neither political nor utopian. This means that when Groys praises his postutopians for illustrating in different ways the indifferent law that art seeks power, he is avoiding any politics of art except perhaps of the most preliminary kind.

The tendency to aggrandize his ideas to the point of emptiness is Groys's besetting vice as a writer, undermining the conceptual oppositions vital to his dialectical arguments. But when he holds out against his mania for generalization, he has suggestive and disturbing things to say not only about Soviet culture but about contemporary capitalist art. Inattentive to individual artworks, he is best at conjuring the spirit of entire institutions and movements. In *Art Power* he shows a surprising appreciation of contemporary museums in general, after characterizing them in *The Total Art of Stalin* as mausoleums of the avant-garde. Today museums offer "practically the only places we can step back from our own present and compare it with other historical eras." This is nearly a truism; it's more typical of Groys's willingness to offend when he argues, in an essay on "Hitler's art theory," that we would possess ampler sense of history if we honored Nazism as possessing a genuine aesthetic. "The ultimate art work," for the painter manqué Hitler, was "the viewer whom heroic politics make into a member of the heroic race." Groys is clearly attracted in principle to art that heroically takes the viewer for its medium.

Groys's inclination towards an art that merges with its public shapes the most interesting essay in *Introduction to Antiphilosophy*, "A Genealogy of Participatory Art," where he makes good on the allusion to Wagner in the title of the Stalin book. The composer's idea of the *Gesamtkunstwerk* or total artwork, he explains, is not to be understood as a multimedia spectacle, but as a forerunner of participatory art. It aims to effect, for audience and artist alike, what Wagner called "the passing over of Egoism into Communism." (Groys is alive to the irony of Richard Wagner renouncing the ego: "One might also claim that . . . this self-abdication . . . grants the author the possibility of controlling the audience.") The lineage of participatory art, defined by incidental resemblance rather than direct ancestry, also threads together Bahktin's theory of carnival; the free-form "happenings" of the 1960s; Warhol's Factory; and the Situationist *dérive* through the streets of Paris. The varieties of participatory art matter less than their common effort "to devalue the symbolic value of art" through the surrender of "personal individuality and authorship to commonality."

As Groys has swung his gaze from East to West some of his critical values have also changed sides. His praise for Western museums is one such reversal; another has to do with the world outside museum walls. Various left-affiliated twentieth-century art movements, from Surrealists to Situationists, sought a mutually transformative encounter between art and daily—especially urban—life. That dream is now dead, thanks to the petrification of contemporary urban life by "the tourist's medusan gaze." "Cities originally came about as projects for the future"; therefore "a genuine city is not only utopian, it is also antitourist." Tourism imposes "a homogeneity bereft of universality." Cities become identical in spite of their cherished differences; their sameness consists in having equally abandoned the universal project of utopia to which they once gave so many local habitations and names. Thus the tourist-citizen finds wherever he goes "the indifferent, utterly privatized life of postcommunism." (Groys might have pointed out that in medieval Europe a city of free citizens, without lords or serfs, was percisely a *commune*.)

A homogeneity bereft of universality might also sum up Groys's view of an international art world which artists, critics, curators, and the authors of press releases more often describe in terms of its irreducible pluralism. Modernism was driven by the continual conquest of new formal territory and abandonment of trampled battlegrounds; beginning perhaps with the extinction of avant-gardes around 1970, art in general and the visual arts in particular have more and more been defined by an omnidirectional spinning out of styles and tendencies, with the cyclicality of fashion rather than the forward charge implied by the term *avant-garde*. Yet it's precisely the contemporary art world's ostensible pluralism that, for Groys, constitutes its secret homogeneity:

> Postmodern taste is by no means as tolerant as it seems . . . [It] in fact rejects everything universal, uniform, repetitive . . . And, of course, the postmodern sensibility strongly dislikes—and *must* dislike—the gray, monotonous, uninspiring look of Communism . . . Communist aesthetics confronts the dominating pluralist, postmodern taste with its universalist, uniform Other . . . What is the origin of this dominating postmodern taste for colorful diversity? . . . It is the taste *formed* by the contemporary market, and it is the taste *for* the market.

There's something attractive about this Hegelian romancing of totality: don't "eclectic," uncoordinated tastes in art often serve to rationalize a failure to think things through in matters of culture? But Groys's argument that the exclusion of Communist drab from the postmodern kaleidoscope gives the lie to neoliberal "diversity" is more impressive as rhetoric than logic. There's nothing contradictory about a pluralist aesthetic disfavoring the idea of an aesthetic dictatorship: every principle is hostile to its own negation. Nor is to "dislike" something necessarily to ban it; the market can offer us Groys's book admiring the total artistry of Stalin. What he says in "Beyond Diversity" is perfectly consistent, except in tone, with standard apologies for liberal capitalism: the marketplace—of art as of ideas—should be unrestricted, and the minimal universalism contained in this sole tenet is the condition of pluralism, not its self-contradiction.

Even so, there will be something persuasive to many gallery-goers in Groys's sense of the paradoxical uniformity of an art world that still rewards the unique style above all else. If we glimpse a lurking void behind the busy surfaces of contemporary art, Groys's best explanation for this lies in *The Communist Postscript*, which barely mentions art. Here Groys attempts to vindicate Soviet communism as philosophy as his earlier book recognized it as a total artwork. By the word *communism*, Groys understands not necessarily common ownership of the means of production but "the project of subordinating the economy to politics in order to allow politics to act freely and sovereignly. The economy functions in the medium of money. It operates with numbers. Politics functions in the medium of language." Thus "the communist revolution is the transcription of society from the medium of money to the medium of language." Capitalism, on the other hand, performs the same operation in reverse, converting all would-be signifiers into mere price signals. The hush of commodification falls over even the most contrary utterance. "Discourses of critique and protest" can "in no respect" be "distinguished from other commodities, which are equally silent—or speak only in self-advertisement."

The meaning of art notoriously exceeds paraphrase. Still, art has enough in common with language that artistic expression today presumably faces the same empty choice between silence and self-advertisement that Groys presents for verbal expression. Art's loss, through universal commodification, of the capacity for transcendent meaning would then explain why the bright palette of contemporary art should seem to pall into common blankness. Only, what can it mean for Groys to say that "so long as humans live under conditions of the capitalist economy they remain fundamentally mute"?

In recent years, Žižek and Badiou have argued that a society dominated by a runaway economic process is nihilistic, inhuman. Humans, after all, are distinguished from other animals, in the classical conception, by our capacity for speech and correspondingly political nature; to subordinate politics to economics is therefore an abdication of humanity. Such an understanding lies behind Badiou's declaration, in *The Communist Hypothesis* (2006), that capitalism "reduces humanity, as far as its collective being is concerned, to animality." Groys makes the same deduction from Aristotelian premises, and in *The Communist Postscript* offers a utopian complement to Badiou's dystopian picture. Only with the full "linguistification of society" by communism would humans "truly become beings who exist in language." The redemption of language through politics would at last permit society to become philosophical, philosophy being the highest and most capacious form of speech.

Groys's vision of communism as the kingdom of philosophy is not only utopian; it is also nostalgic for Stalin's Soviet

Union, which "understood itself literally as a state governed by philosophy alone." (This contradicts the idea that the USSR was organized principally along aesthetic lines— unless art and philosophy are, as sometimes seems the case in Groys, two names for the one thing.) The reigning Soviet philosophy was the revision of historical materialism that Stalin called dialectical materialism, and for Groys Stalin's intellectual advance over his predecessors consists of two moves: first, dialectical materialism puts language above both society's economic base and the cultural superstructure to which language might appear to belong; second, dialectical materialism can better grasp the world in its totality than other philosophies, thanks to a unique tolerance for paradox. The defect of ordinary formal logic is to rule out paradox, while the traditional or pre-Stalinist dialectic "temporalizes paradox," seeing what Engels called the unity of opposites as produced over time: two contradictory propositions can't be equally true at one and the same instant, but the dynamic totality of history may grant them both their momentary truth. Dialectical materialism by contrast holds that life is defined by "the figure of paradox," in the sense of the simul- taneous validity of contradictory propositions. This means the Stalinist "revival of the Platonic dream of the kingdom of philosophers" didn't require in theory the totalitarian rule it excused in practice. Communism, "distinguished from a Platonic state insofar as it was the duty of every individual to be a philosopher, not just the duty of the governing class," doesn't ideally compel "any quieting of conflicts; on the contrary, it promises to intensify them."

It's impossible to know why Groys has stubbornly upheld Stalinism as the model of a society that grants art its due power or redeems for a language a philosophical significance today cashiered by capitalism. Trotsky, for one, also imagined, more explicitly than Stalin, a comprehensive aestheticization of society. "The wall will fall not only between art and industry," he wrote in *Literature and Revolution* (1924), "but simultaneously between art and nature." And if Stalin's dialectical materialism implied, as Groys says, that socialism should foster rather than restrict the expression of conflicting views, Trotsky was again more forthright: "The powerful force of competition which, in bourgeois society, has the character of market competition, will not disappear in a Socialist society, but, to use the language of psychoanalysis, will be sublimated, that is, will assume a higher and more fertile form. There will be the struggle for one's opinion, for one's project, for one's taste." Trotsky's chapter on a "communist policy towards art" includes a proviso later contravened by socialist realism: "the domain of art is not one in which the party is called to command." The total art foreseen by Trotsky—in which art, no longer "merely 'pretty' without relationship to anything else," becomes "the most progressive building of life in every field"—resembles that described in *The Total Art of Stalinism* except for being so much more democratic in spirit, with an aesthetic signature of complexity and variety rather than uniformity. Groys never mentions Trotsky's vision. Bukharin, another of Stalin's victims, likewise goes unnoted in his book on Soviet philosophy. Their fates are two of many to suggest that the basic rhetorical "figure" of the Soviet Union wasn't philosophical paradox so much as tragic irony.

Some of Groys's peculiar attachment to Stalin may come from his childhood in Leningrad. But the logic of his work invites another explanation. If it's true today that "every protest is fundamentally senseless, for in capitalism language itself functions as a commodity," a book asking you to buy the idea of Stalinism as the pinnacle of modern art or philosophy nevertheless stands out a little from the rest of the wares in the museum gift shop. Groys's appreciation of socialist realism and dialectical materialism as formal advances—almost heroically perverse in light of Stalinist denunciations of decadent "formalism"—has been, if nothing else, a momentary stay against the incorporation of his own work into the glut of distinctions without a difference that for him constitutes the contemporary art world.

Even so, Groys's work ultimately reproduces the logic of unmeaning sameness he ascribes to capital. His most representative modern artist, after Stalin, is Marcel Duchamp, who shared with Stalin, if nothing else, the impulse to blur the boundaries between art and non-art. Duchamp's readymades, whereby a urinal has only to be mounted on a wall to become an art object, inspire the "readymade (anti)philosophy" proposed in Groys's latest book, which produces "truth effects" in "the same way in which 'aesthetic experience' is produced in the case of artistic readymades: it can be attached to any possible object." For Groys, the virtue of (anti)philosophy, with its tellingly optional prefix, is that unlike traditional "command-giving" philosophy it opens up "an imaginary perspective of limitless life, in which all decisions of life lose their urgency, so that the opposition between carrying out and rejecting a command dissolves in the infinite play of life possibilities." This sounds less like politics, a zone virtually defined by ineluctable decisions and sovereign commands, than like clinical descriptions of catatonic schizo-phrenia, in which complete inanition is the condition for simultaneously holding incompatible ideas of one's self and the world. The aesthetics of Soviet "life-building" and the Duchampian readymade—one an exercise of power, the other a trick of perception—can only be reconciled at the expense of the distinctive properties of each. Groys's way of rhyming Stalinism with solipsism, as when he writes that "the death of totalitarianism has made totalitarians of us all," is the sort of thing to make you wonder whether his work isn't an elaborate prank.

A more generous, not to say historical materialist, reading might see in Groys's particular combination of stridency and vagueness something of the general predicament of art and criticism these days. How can the artist or critic provoke a reaction when he finds himself surrounded by the jaded inhabitants of the art world? More clearly than any ideologi-cal alteration or formal dynamic, a basic change of social situation marks off postmodern (or anti-utopian or neolib-eral) art from the modern art of socialist or capitalist coun-tries. The world of so-called high art is more than ever sepa-rate from the lives of the governed or the governing classes, and art's gain in autonomy has come at great cost to any political relevance. In Moscow in the 1980s, the poet Vsevolod

Nekrasov wrote some lines rhyming Groys's surname with that of the German artist Joseph Beuys and an imperative form of the Russian word for *fear*. In Ainsley Morse and Bela Shayevich's English rendering:

> don't oh boy Beuys
> but if you gotta fret
> forget Beuys, get
>
> fed up with gross Groys

It seems that Nekrasov felt Groys had betrayed artists like himself by defining them before the public as "conceptualists" in his 1979 essay "Moscow Romantic Conceptualism." More evident is that in New York or Moscow today it's much harder for the art critic to inspire fretting or fear: a difficulty that may account for the both the froth of outrageousness and the undertow of emptiness in Groys's work. Reading him, I sometimes thought of an exchange between the comedian Will Ferrell and his costar in the Hollywood male figure-skating film *Blades of Glory* (2007), a mostly boring comedy occasionally startled into wit at its own and its viewer's expense. When Ferrell's character insists on choreographing a pairs routine to "My Humps," the anatomically puzzling hit song about "lady humps" by the Black Eyed Peas, his partner complains that he has no idea what the song means. "No one knows what it means," Ferrell replies. "But it's provocative."

Is something like this the secret motto enfolding the art of neoliberalism together with the work of its desperate critics?

Not long ago I was at MoMA, where I paid $25 to see, among other things, a half dozen Malevich canvasses. I also saw hundreds of people surrounding the actress Tilda Swinton, asleep in a glass box. No one knew what this meant, but it was provocative—unless its apparent meaninglessness was just the reason that it wasn't.

It marked one kind of dead end for left art criticism when Adorno argued that modern art constituted the sole remaining preserve of radical politics. For him, modernism testified at once, in its agony, to the badness of existing society and, in its very abstractness, to the enduring possibility of a good society whose blank potentiality was all that could be known of it. Today it's clear that, blessed with official approval, even the most refractory modernism could just as well ornament the existing order as intimate a different one: Adorno glimpsed this possibility when he noticed Kafka's novels among the customary furnishings of the middle-class household. Groys, faced with a capitalist art world liberated from the rest of society into splendid irrelevance, has tried in different ways to imagine, not an art autonomous from society, but an art through which society itself becomes autonomous: a participatory total art. But the effort arrives at its own dead end, from a direction opposite to Adorno's.

A theoretical communist with a more materialist outlook would see that a substantial socialization of art must accompany any worthwhile—that is, democratic or participatory—aestheticization of society. For now, Groys's eccentrically communist vision of a "new sensibility for radical art" can only ratify the gulf between the specialized art world and the general public that he would like see closed.

His work is nevertheless an occasion to remember, amid the tentative revival of Marxism over recent years, that a revolution in culture was also part of the socialist project. Even today the experience of art continues to radicalize many sensibilities more decisively, if obscurely, than political argument. Groys's favored word *power*, however, used with any connotation of force, is the wrong one for this or any other effect of what we call powerful art: the essence of pity and terror, or mirth, recognition, gratitude or indignation, is to be unavailable to compulsion. As for the aesthetics of a utopia worthy of the name, it's impossible to say what the art of an economically just, politically free, and ecologically viable social formation might look like. It would be interesting, not to say beautiful, to find out.

August 2013

A Guide to Further Reading

Even a fully postmodernized First World society will not lack young people whose temperament and values are genuinely left ones and embrace visions of radical social change repressed by a business society. The dynamics of such commitment are derived not from the reading of the "Marxist classics," but rather from the objective experience of social reality and the way in which one isolated cause or issue, one specific form of injustice, cannot be fulfilled or corrected without eventually drawing the entire web of interrelated social levels together into a totality, which then demands the intervention of a politics of social transformation.

I first came upon these words (which are echoed in the introduction to this volume) in 1996, in the conclusion to *Late Marxism*, Fredric Jameson's study of Theodor Adorno. This was an ironic place for me to find the importance of reading downplayed, when the living writer who had done most to solidify my initial sense of myself as a radical or leftist was

Jameson himself and, among figures from the past, the most important to me in this respect was none other than Adorno. Today my admiration for these writers is at once more qualified and deeper: for example, Jameson's deliberate neglect of political questions and Adorno's strictures against utopian imaginings no longer strike me as useful principles, at the same time that my own efforts to write about cultural matters without losing sight of economic reality has increased my appreciation for both men's work. Anyway, a Marxist's education never ends. For me, reading and experience, experience and reading, have sometimes corrected and sometimes corroborated each other. At other times the value of reading has seemed to lie precisely in the capacity of texts, and works of history and theory in particular, to capture aspects of the world unavailable to thought. With that in mind, it may be worth listing a few books against which readers can test against their own experience and ideas.

The foregoing essays can obviously enough be taken to recommend David Harvey's *Limits of Capital*, Robert Brenner's *Economics of Global Turbulence*, and David Graeber's *Debt: The First 5,000 Years* as basic texts of our economic moment. Other important titles by the same writers include Harvey's *Brief Introduction to Neoliberalism* (2007), an indispensable book on the subject it names, not least for stressing the decisive role of the state in an era whose neoliberal rhetoric has minimized government's role in capital accumulation; the essays by Brenner, in a contentious collection by various authors called *The Brenner Debate* (1985), on the English roots of a European capitalism that launched a revolution in agricultural productivity strikingly in contrast to the industrial slowdown that Brenner finds in recent decades; and Graeber's *Direct Action: An Ethnography* (2009), the best contemporary account I know of the moral allure of anarchism. As for Jameson himself, the place to start—or return to him—may be *The Cultural Turn* (1998), a selection of fundamental writings on postmodernism, although my favorites among his books happen to be *Marxism and Form* (1974), a stylistically magnificent introduction to a half dozen twentieth-century dialectical thinkers from Lukács to Sartre, and *The Political Unconscious* (1982), which offers at once a theoretical vindication of Marxist criticism and, through historically situated readings of classic novels by Balzac and Conrad among others, an exemplary demonstration of the practice.

My discussions of Slavoj Žižek and Boris Groys differ from the other pieces in this collection in that they aren't exactly appreciations. Still, these writers have provoked my admiration as well as antagonism. Žižek's *Everything You Always Wanted to Know about Lacan . . . But Were Afraid to Ask Hitchock* (1993)—to mention just one of his dozens of books, many of them unopened by me—makes for a lucid introduction to Lacan's thought that will also probably change how any reader watches movies and TV in a culture dominated by commercially produced audiovisuals. Groys, in *The Communist Postscript*, bracingly imagines a different and more verbal form of society, no longer ruled by money (or images) but governed, far more than today, through language and even philosophy. These books might be read alongside Guy Debord's classic *Society of the Spectacle* (1967), a brilliant series of aphorisms on postwar capitalism as an exploitative social relationship frozen and estranged into images.

Naturally there are many other writers than these who have influenced my (evolving and incomplete) conception of capitalism past and present, and of the alternate order we may aim at. I'll mention sixteen, some Marxist and others not, rather than pretend to draw up some comprehensive syllabus. The number is as arbitrary as the selection is personal. Arranged in a certain order like books on a shelf, this selection of their books can nevertheless suggest something of the arc of historical capitalism as well as compensate for my neglect of political and ecological questions in a set of essays that have concentrated on economics and culture.

If it has been difficult for us over the past generation to imagine how one mode of production—in our case, a global capitalism reliant on fossil fuels and state power—might give way to another, this impasse owes something to our generally impoverished idea of how such transitions took place in the past. Perry Anderson's *Passages from Antiquity to Feudalism* (1974) traces the gradual dissolution of classical slavery as a mode of production and the emergence in medieval Europe of that method of generating and controlling an economic surplus known as feudalism. Its sequel, *Lineages of the Absolutist State* (also 1974), analyzes the system of modern states first erected on the basis of European feudalism, and in the process makes a strong case for the state as a constitutive element of later feudalism and of capitalism from the outset. These brilliantly composed works of comparative history also pay a consistent if never theorized attention to the ecological difficulties that various precapitalist social formations encountered.

In *The Origin of Capitalism: A Longer View* (2002), Ellen Meiksins Wood offers a clear and concise argument, closely following Brenner's, that the beginnings of our own distinctive mode of production lie in the novel "market-dependency" of sixteenth-century English farmers. Earlier societies had sometimes made extensive use of markets, but without forcing property-owners and laborers alike to rely upon markets for their whole livelihood, as they—or we—still do today. The long agricultural boom unleashed by this change would have by itself set English and western European living standards apart from those of most of the rest of the world—but not from all of it, as Kenneth Pomeranz points out in *The Great Divergence: China, Europe, and the Making of the Modern World Economy* (2001). For several centuries prior to the nineteenth, Japan and coastal China enjoyed a prosperity equal to or greater than England's. The great divergence between western European and east Asian fortunes first came about through British exploitation of "coal and colonies," in Pomeranz's alliterative formulation: an ecological revolution to complement the economic one described by Wood.

Eric Hobsbawm's tetralogy of modern history—*The Age of Revolution* (1962), *The Age of Capital* (1975), and *The Age of Empire* (1987) on the "long nineteenth century" from 1789 to 1914, and *The Age of Extremes* (1994) on "the short twentieth century" from 1914 to 1991—lacks the theoretical single-mindedness of Pomeranz or Wood but unveils as rich a mural of two hundred years of industrial capitalism, in its economy, politics, culture, and science, as any single author could produce, besides being a continuous pleasure to read. The temporal scope of Giovanni Arrighi's *Long Twentieth Century* (1994) and *Adam Smith in Beijing* (2007) is even greater. These books discover the springs of capitalism not in sixteenth-century English agriculture but in the international finance pioneered by northern Italian city states of the fifteenth, while discerning a possible terminus to capitalism in a "non-capitalist market economy" of the twenty-first. The overall effect is to convey the shape of capitalism as one long integral process, culminating for now in a crisis that Arrighi (who died in 2009) anticipated in his discussion of financialization of the American economy.

Potential solutions to the crisis are easier to find in economic theory than economic history. John Maynard Keynes's classic *General Theory of Employment, Interest and Money* (1936) offers not just a diagnosis of capitalist crisis— "The outstanding faults of the economic society in which we live are its failure to provide for full employment and its arbitrary and inequitable distribution of wealth and incomes"— but a partial remedy for it. One Keynesian medicine is "a substantial socialization of investment." *The General Theory* is also a masterpiece of tone, by turns sarcastic, sweetly reasonable, wistful, haughty, and impassioned: proof, in all, that economists needn't write deadly prose. The works of Keynes's follower Hyman Minsky, particularly *John Maynard Keynes* (1975) and *Stabilizing an Unstable Economy* (1986), can't be recommended on their literary merits but do suggest, in their advocacy of large-scale public investment, how

Keynesian and socialist responses to the present crisis might converge.

Keynesianism, however, possesses no explanation for the reluctance of governments to adopt economic policies favoring the common good—which is after all not the object of capitalist societies. Lenin's *State and Revolution* (1917), a famous book more mentioned than read, offers a useful reminder that capitalist states necessarily serve capitalist interests, as well a vision (travestied by the state Lenin founded) of an egalitarian public carrying out its own administration rather than delegate the task to unaccountable officials. Still, Lenin's crude account of the interrelationship of governments and capitalism lacks the subtlety, lucidity, and consequent persuasiveness of Ralph Miliband's *The State in Capitalist Society* (1967), which (much like Anderson's typology of feudal monarchies in *Lineages of The Absolutist State*) shows how the dominant class increases its power by giving up some of that power to the state. Antonio Gramsci's earlier *Prison Notebooks* (1948–51) still contain perhaps the most intelligent discussion available of strategies for the conquest of power in wealthy countries with democratic protocols. Together these books insist on the necessity of political strategy and organizing, without which the left's finest policy proposals are a dead letter and capitalist crisis a blown opportunity.

The terrain on which we need to organize is of course very different from that of Lenin or Gramsci, in part because capitalism appears to be coming up against ecological limits invisible in their day. *Something New Under the Sun: An*

Environmental History of the Twentieth-Century World (2001) by J. R. McNeill gives an alarming (though not alarmist) overview of a profligate century in which state socialism compiled an environmental record arguably worse than capitalism's. A twenty-first-century Marxism has be green if it's to be at all. In *Marx's Ecology: Materialism and Nature* (2000), John Bellamy Foster presents Marx and Engels as properly ecological thinkers whose contemporary concerns about soil exhaustion imply a general concept of the "metabolic rift" between humanity and nature opened up by capitalism.

Herman Daly's *Steady-State Economics* (1991) imagines, with a sort of visionary simplicity, what the basic institutions of a metabolically or environmentally sound society might be like. These include not only checks on resource depletion but mechanisms for radically narrowing income inequality. Daly, like Keynes, is no Marxist—and an economist whose conclusions are essential for Marxists to reckon with. Meanwhile, the outlines of an ecological socialism can be glimpsed in two books by André Gorz, a Marxist opposed to what he regarded as the overemphasis on work in Marx himself: *Critique of Economic Reason* (1990) and *Capitalism, Socialism, Ecology* (1991). For Gorz, a better society would not eliminate but curb the economic rationality that today—irrationally—places the well-being of any individual person, as well as that of earthly nature as a whole, at the mercy of the market.

In *Revolution at Point Zero: Housework, Reproduction, and Feminist Struggle* (2012), Silvia Federici poses in her own way the fundamental question of the ideal dimensions of the economy. Among Federici's potent arguments is that so-called reproductive labor, done preponderantly by women, deserves the same sort of monetary compensation as the "productive" labor of workers on the job market. The idea bears some resemblance to the "basic communism" proposed by the (non-Marxist) American polymath Lewis Mumford, in *Technics and Civilization* (1934), according to which a minimum income is due all members of society.

Writing in the midst of the Depression, Mumford was still admirably capable of utopian accents, and concluded his magisterial survey of technological developments over five centuries with a call to "socialize creation":

> The creative life, in all its manifestations, is necessarily a social product. It grows with the aid of transitions and techniques maintained and transmitted by society at large, and neither tradition nor product can remain the sole possession of the scientist or the artist or the philosopher, still less of the privileged groups that, under capitalist conventions, so largely support them ... The essential task of all sound economic activity is to produce a state in which creation will be a common fact in all experience.

The passage suggests that the materially durable physical culture imagined by Mumford—we might today call it environmentally sustainable—needn't rule out creativity. On the contrary, an economy no longer beholden to growth, to the attainment of profits above all, might be far more hospitable to human development.

These words also make explicit one of the premises of the Marxist tradition at its best: the creative work of social transformation is mainly the task of amateurs, not experts. That is something to keep in mind while reading, and not only then.